W9-CPY-511

GETTING HONEST WITH GOD

Praying As If
God Really Listens

MARK LITTLETON

InterVarsity Press
Downers Grove, Illinois

InterVarsity Press
P.O. Box 1400, Downers Grove, IL 60515-1426
World Wide Web: www.ivpress.com
E-mail: mail@ivpress.com

InterVarsity Press® is the book-publishing division of InterVarsity Christian Fellowship/USA®, a student movement active on campus at hundreds of universities, colleges and schools of nursing in the United States of America, and a member movement of the International Fellowship of Evangelical Students. For information about local and regional activities, write Public Relations Dept., InterVarsity Christian Fellowship/USA, 6400 Schroeder Rd., P.O. Box 7895, Madison, WI 53707-7895, or visit the IVCF website at <www.ivcf.org>.

All Scripture quotations, unless otherwise indicated, are taken from the Holy Bible, New International Version®. NIV®. Copyright ©1973, 1978, 1984 by International Bible Society. Used by permission of Zondervan Publishing House. All rights reserved.

Cover design: Cindy Kiple

Cover image: lady: Mel Curtis/Getty Images
black man: Steve Vaccariello/Getty Images
white man: Getty Images

ISBN 0-8308-2385-9

Printed in the United States of America ∞

Library of Congress Cataloging-in-Publication Data

Littleton, Mark R., 1950-
  Getting honest with God: praying as if God really listens/Mark
Littleton.
    p. cm.
  ISBN 0-8308-2385-9 (pbk.: alk. paper)
  1. Prayer—Christianity. I. Title
  BV210.3 .L58 2003
  248.3'2—dc21

                                                                          2002152084

| P | 17 | 16 | 15 | 14 | 13 | 12 | 11 | 10 | 9 | 8 | 7 | 6 | 5 | 4 | 3 | 2 | 1 |
| Y | 15 | 14 | 13 | 12 | 11 | 10 | 09 | 08 | 07 | 06 | 05 | 04 | 03 |

To Jeanette, who keeps me smiling.

CONTENTS

Introduction 9

1. THE PRAYER FOR INTIMACY
   God Longs for Us to Know Him 11

2. THE PRAYER IN ANGER
   God Knows How to Deal with It 28

3. THE PRAYER OF RELINQUISHMENT
   Surrender All to God 47

4. THE PRAYER OUT OF DOUBT
   God Will Give You What You Need 65

5. THE PRAYER OF DEEP DISAPPOINTMENT
   Remember, You Aren't Home Yet 80

6. THE PRAYER WITH BOLDNESS
   God Will Act 98

7. THE PRAYER OF WEAK FAITH
   Just Admit It 112

8. THE PRAYER FOR HEALING
   God Knows Precisely What You Need 128

9. THE ARGUING PRAYER
   Persuade God Otherwise 145

INTRODUCTION

At FIRST IT SEEMS LIKE A NO-BRAINER. Honest with God? Of course. Why would anyone attempt to be dishonest with him who is all-knowing?

But I'm not talking about being deceitful with God the way a person might be with a boss, sibling or spouse. This book isn't about white lies or even huge whoppers. It's more about larger issues: anger, discouragement, doubt and lack of faith.

These are issues that we all face every day but that many of us find it difficult to talk to God about. After all, if we have doubts, misgivings or fears, isn't God the last person we want to tell this to? Isn't it silly to tell God we have those issues when the very act of prayer demonstrates that we really don't have them—at least not enough to keep us from praying?

And anger—who are *we* to be angry with God? Angry with ourselves, sure. With others, definitely. But with God? Couldn't he simply incinerate us on the spot if we got huffy with him?

In the end getting honest with God is about these very things. Is it ever okay to be angry with God and let him know that—have a face-off with him? Can we experience genuine doubts and then have the audacity to reveal them to God, the very One we doubt? Is it ever all right to tell God we simply don't believe he'll answer the prayer we bring to him? I have asked these questions of God many times throughout my life—and I want to share my journey with you.

This book will speak to situations that, I believe, wrench the very guts of our faith in Christ and yet that, when expressed and worked through, can bring tremendous results in our relationship with him. In each chapter we'll look at a biblical character who dealt with such issues. How they handled them and how they came out at the end provides powerful insight into our own circumstances.

I hope you'll read expecting your friendship with God to reach a new level. I know writing this book and wrestling with these issues has enabled me to grow greatly in my fellowship with Christ and to love him more deeply.

1

THE PRAYER FOR INTIMACY
God Longs for Us to Know Him

The next day John was there again with two of his disciples. When he saw Jesus passing by, he said, "Look, the Lamb of God!"

When the two disciples heard him say this, they followed Jesus. Turning around, Jesus saw them following and asked, "What do you want?"

They said, "Rabbi" (which means Teacher), "where are you staying?"
"Come," he replied, "and you will see."

So they went and saw where he was staying, and spent that day with him. It was about the tenth hour.

JOHN 1:35-39

TWO FERVENT DISCIPLES have followed John the Baptist for some time, perhaps months, maybe years. They revere him. They come to hear his impassioned messages with expectation and a sense of destiny. John would be the prophet to usher in the Messiah, the One these two men looked for, hoping for a new life, a new universe.

One day John stops in the middle of a message. He stares at a man before him. They have an earnest, concerned exchange. Then John baptizes him.

As the man pushes up from the water, the sky rips open. A white dove plummets and lights on the stranger's head. Then a commanding, thunderous voice speaks out of nowhere: "This is my Son, whom I love; with him I am well pleased" (Matthew 3:17). Moments later the dust settles. The sky closes. All is quiet.

The man whom John has baptized trudges out of the water, through the crowd. All stare. John himself gazes after the man, then bellows out, "Look, the Lamb of God, who takes away the sin of the world!" (John 1:29).

The "Lamb" disappears into the distance. People rush to John. "What was that all about?" "Who was he?" "What should we do?"

John explains that this man is the Lamb of God who has come to take away sin for all time, the one living and true sacrifice, whom all the temple sacrifices foreshadowed. This is the One who will accomplish true redemption. He doesn't say so, but the minds of his hearers all must leap to the question *Could this be the awaited Messiah?*

As John talks, these two disciples glance at one another with wide eyes. They also wonder, *Could this be the one? What should we do?*

At this point, nothing. The Lamb of God has disappeared into the wilderness. The moment has passed, lost for all time. The disciples decide to wait, see what happens, see if the Lamb returns.

Two months later (after Jesus' temptation in the wilderness), the Lamb of God returns to the Jordan River area. John offers more pronouncements. The mystery deepens.

Finally the Lamb appears a third time. John again shouts, in effect, "This is the Lamb of God, people. Are you listening?"

This time they are ready. They gather their bedrolls and follow Jesus back into the rocky, barren wilderness. They want to find out if he truly is the Savior, the Messiah sent to bring a new kingdom.

As they hurry to catch up, they study the man, the way he walks and carries himself, how tall he is. They begin to think he just doesn't look like the mighty King come to rescue Israel from slavery and destruction. He looks too ordinary.

But before they decide to forget the whole thing, the Lamb of God surprises them. He whips around and says, "What do you want?" (John 1:38). It's not, "Who are you?" or "What can you do for me?" or "Why are you following me?" No, Jesus does something far greater, something so beautiful it's stunning. He gives these two inquirers a chance to ask bluntly and directly the issues filling their minds.

Isn't that just like Jesus? He never wastes a moment dancing around an issue. He goes right to the heart of any matter—with us, with everyone. That's how he deals with Nicodemus in John 3 and the woman at the well in John 4. All throughout the Gospel of John we see Jesus plunging to the center of every issue, every conversation in a blunt way that is startling.

It's a good trait, isn't it? Jesus didn't come to earth to dither around. He had three years of inspired ministry ahead of him, and he couldn't spend it making small talk. But now, how would the two men respond to his blunt question?

You might expect the disciples to say, "Rabbi, John said you're the Lamb of God. Are you?" They didn't. Maybe that was too direct. Try: "Rabbi, what's your name?" or "Where are you from?" But that's not what they say. What blurts from their lips is the question "Rabbi, where are you staying?"

What kind of a question is that? It's almost too forward, too personal. Maybe they half expected to find Jesus returning to some outpost in the wilderness, the fortress from which he would launch the juggernaut that would accomplish the awesome plan of redemption. Or maybe they expected him to lead them right to Herod's temple and there declare the arrival of the Anointed One. Or maybe it was just the first thing that leaped into their minds. I suspect they were both so flabbergasted that Jesus spoke to them first that they didn't know what to say.

The disciples' question is surprising, but Jesus gives an even more astonishing answer: "Come, and you will see" (John 1:39). It's an open invitation. *All right,* Jesus might have thought, *you two don't know what you want. Then I'll give you the time you need to find out.*

They follow Jesus to his lodging place and spend the whole night with him there. What do you think they talked about? I would guess anything and everything they'd ever wanted to know about God, life, the world, the future, human history, redemption—you name it.

By the time they return home the next morning, Jesus has convinced them he is the Messiah. How do we know? Because that is what Andrew (one of the two disciples present) told his brother Simon (soon to be renamed Peter) in the next passage in John 1.

MEETING THE LORD OF LIFE

Could meeting and talking with the Lord of life have been that simple? Is God really that approachable? Yes. And why not? When you think about it, those two men could have been you or me. They weren't famous, rich or powerful. They didn't call ahead and make an appointment. Neither had a claim on Christ. But they did have the ordinary need to know if he was who John said he was. So Jesus offered them a ripe opportunity to spend a day with the Ruler of the universe.

Why? Because they were interested enough to come after him? Sure, that's good enough. But I don't think that's the reason.

Did Jesus invite them to his home just because they showed up? After all, that was rather risky. These two probably expected the Anointed One to reside someplace much better than the average Israelite hovel. A palace, perhaps. Or a least an estate. After all, he was going to rule the world. Rulers don't live in shacks down by the tracks. So this was a very risky answer. Showing these two earnest men his earthy, plain home could burst two very fragile balloons for good. But that still doesn't answer the question.

Why did Jesus invite these men to his house where they might sit, stay and sup well into the evening, where a moment of vulnerability could blow everything? Because they were future disciples? Perhaps. Because Jesus was beginning the ministry that would inflame the Hebrew world? Maybe. Because Jesus saw who and what they would become? I think it was all of that. But at least one thing more: because they followed him on John's directive and asked. They asked!

It's a little astonishing, isn't it? Because they *asked?* What kind of reason is that?

Think about it. Undoubtedly many people were at the Jordan that day. Presumably multitudes heard John's words. John was the Billy

Graham of Judea in those days. So people flocked to him. But only two cranked up the nerve to go and find out what Jesus was all about. To ask.

It's quite a monumental truth when you think about it. How many of us will ever get an invitation to the White House? Who among us, if any, could walk into Congress and win the ear of any political mover and shaker without a famous name and tremendous clout to pave the way? What human can stride into the throne room of royalty and say, "Hey, let's have tea"? A very select few. Probably not you or me. But this Jesus invites these two bumpkins into his home—and also into his heart.

THE GOD WHO IS APPROACHABLE

Did you ever notice how Scripture repeatedly reveals that God, the Creator of the universe, the King of kings and Owner of everything, wants people to come to him and share everything with him? All we have to do is ask. Incredible!

Rosalind Rinker said in her book *Prayer: Conversing with God* that "prayer is a dialogue between two persons who love each other." What a perfect illustration of this situation! Christ already cared about these two men, and they were beginning to love him. Jesus craves the conversation and interaction of prayer, and he loves us to simply ask for things—whether it's needs, fears, ideas or questions we're struggling with. To ask!

Getting honest with God means recognizing this astonishing truth about him: he wants us to come to him, anytime, anywhere, and solicit him for anything. He wants to converse with us. He wants a relationship with us, a friendship. That means coming to him and asking him about the great questions of the universe. That means inviting him to work in our lives and change us. That calls for simple talk late into the evening.

Why is this? Why does the simple act of asking move God to action? To ask demonstrates need, dependence, humility. It exhibits faith. You can't see God. You can't hear him. But when you ask, you demonstrate genuine faith, the one thing he most values in believers. You believe he's there and he rewards those who seek him, as Hebrews 11:6 says.

God likes—no, *loves*—the asking attitude because it lets him be God and lets us be us. So in Scripture, God frequently invites us to ask him something, anything. "Call to me and I will answer you and tell you great and unsearchable things you do not know" (Jeremiah 33:3). What greater invitation do we need? He calls to us to come to him and ask anything, and he'll tell us the secrets of the universe.

How many people the world over have wanted to know the answers to simple questions like "Is there a God? Where is he? Who am I? Why am I here?" God wants us simply to ask, and he will answer quickly (though "quickly" means different things to him than to us).

Another verse freighted with promise says, "I will do whatever you ask in my name" (John 14:13). Does this mean we can ask for anything? *Anything?* Our skeptical minds tell us there has to be more to it. Surely we can't ask for anything. "A million dollars by tomorrow night"? "The most beautiful woman on earth as my wife by next week"?

Certainly we can't make frivolous or selfish requests and expect answers. James said, "When you ask, you do not receive, because you ask with wrong motives, that you may spend what you get on your pleasures" (James 4:3).

Then what made Jesus say yes to these two disciples of John? Because they were asking for something Jesus always says yes to: the desire to know him intimately, personally, openly.

Ask for the things of this world, and God may take several years before he answers. But ask for the things of God, that is, the desire to know him and be with him and become forever friends with him, and God will always, *always* say yes. After all, didn't he tell us in Psalm 37:4, "Delight yourself in the LORD and he will give you the desires of your heart"? Isn't that an invitation to, in the name of his kingdom, reach your dreams and achieve stupendous goals you never thought possible?

The disciples wanted something specific from Jesus: to know if he really was the One, the Lord of lords and King of kings. Beyond that, if he was, they wanted to know him intimately, face to face, man to man, as friends and followers and disciples.

Lest we think this is a slight thing, simply wanting to know who Jesus was and what he wants to do in our world, I have to say: isn't that the most important question in all of life? If we don't get that one settled, we could end up weeping and gnashing our teeth for all eternity. If we don't get that settled, we could go through life without the greatest Friend and Helper at our side to guide us in triumphing through life. If we don't get this issue worked out, we could end up beaten down and burned out with no in-depth relationships and no real sense of why we're here on planet earth to begin with. Knowing Jesus is the beginning of everything else.

Getting honest with God means getting honest about the most basic truths in life. We're not talking about knowing him in a cursory way, being able to list a few facts about him. "He was born in a stable, and he was a great healer and miracle worker, and he died a horrible death." True, but that's not knowing and relating and living with him.

Let me suggest several ways we can begin to know him that illustrate getting honest with God in an understandable way.

KNOWING CHRIST SEEKER TO SAVIOR

The first relationship any of us ever has with Jesus Christ is the same as for the two disciples at the Jordan—we are seekers. The disciples wanted to know the truth about our world, life, death, the future, forgiveness and everything else. To get those questions answered and to know the truth is one of the greatest experiences anyone in this world can have. Jesus is the Savior we seek, the One who will take us out of the world one day and put us in that perfect environment we've all longed for. He is our Savior from sin, from death, from hopelessness and from turning into a wasted, useless human being.

I remember when I had not yet met the Lord of the universe. I was in college, sitting under some the most learned professors I have ever met. I studied in depth about all kinds of things—physics, biology, the great Romantic poets—and I piled up a hulking mound of knowledge that seemed vast to me at the time. But in my heart I knew something was missing.

I pondered the issue often and soon realized what it was: I didn't know why I was on earth, who God was (if he existed) and what happened when you died. Those questions tore at my heart nearly every day. The issue of death really felled me. I just did not have a clue what happens when you die. Where do you go? Do you just cease to exist? What about heaven and hell?

I knew enough to believe that if there was a hell, I was probably a prime candidate for residency there. Heaven, if it existed, seemed out of the question for me, even if I took the standard course humans believe—if my good deeds outweigh my bad deeds, I'll go to heaven. I knew my good deeds were few and far between, while my bad deeds—using drugs, cruising on alcohol and engaging in illicit sex—happened just about daily.

The worst part of it was that no one else I knew seemed to know the answers either. In my fraternity house I constantly asked questions of my friends and brothers. Many said, "What does it matter? It won't solve anything." One even said, "I believe we are chemical reactions. Everything that happens inside us is produced by chemistry." It worried me. I knew deep down that life had to be more than that.

One day a friend told me I needed to become a Christian. I didn't really know what I believed at the time, but I knew I didn't practice anything truly Christian. I didn't go to church. I had been raised in a church, but as far as I could tell, it hadn't done me a bit of good. I asked this friend what a Christian was. He told me, "It's not just going to church or anything like that. It's something inside you. It changes you. You can see it in their eyes."

"What's in their eyes?"

He didn't know. "They look different, like a fire burns in their eyes, like they have hope and joy and life, real life."

I hiked into the bathroom to stare into the mirror at my eyes, wondering what was missing.

I didn't give up, though, and one day someone directed me to Hal Lindsey's book *The Late Great Planet Earth*. Lindsey's words ignited me. For the first time I found something that seemed true, that spoke to me where I was with my struggles. For months afterward I mulled on Lindsey's words, and in August 1972, through a conversation with another friend, I trusted Christ.

Wow, that was a jolt! The next day, I saw as with new eyes. I suddenly stared on the world as if I'd never seen it before, with its sin and its sickness and people's mean treatment of one another, but also the glory of it—the beauty of a sunset, the power of friendship, the joy of intimacy. Best of all was that I realized I now knew God. It was an uncanny feeling, knowing this Person who had suddenly broken through the veil of my consciousness. He seemed almost tangible, as if any moment he might burst through the door and sit down with me on my bed. I talked with him and I "felt" him listening. I also "heard" him talking to me—quietly, gently, but in a way that was more real than any other sounds around me.

I was startled beyond words. For the first time in my life, I felt secure. I wasn't worried or afraid about death anymore, nor worried that I might go to hell. I knew who I was, what I was supposed to do and where I would go if I died. My mind teemed with truth I'd never experienced before, and it all seemed so plain, so obvious. How had I missed these realities for so long?

More important, how did I know these truths? For a simple reason: because I knew Jesus. The answer to life's questions is not Einstein's mathematical theorem of energy and mass. It is not a four-point plan from a self-help book. It's Jesus. Himself. The one and only. Being with him, knowing him, conversing with him—that's how we learn the answers about everything else. Ultimately it's he—his presence, his friendship—that is riveting and beautiful beyond understanding.

Do you realize how many poets, philosophers, writers, men, women and children struggle with the great questions of life and never find answers? Do you realize how great it is to know personally, to actually be friends with the God of the universe? One of my professors used to say, "I hope you never recover from it."

If you are a Christian, you are linked spiritually with the God of the universe. He knows you completely and he loves you through and through. You're a member of his family. You have all the rights and privileges of a member of the Royal Family of royal families. If someone were to pop up to heaven and ask God, "Hey, do you know So-and-so?" referring to you, God would say, "Yes, I have So-and-so's picture right here in my wallet!"

People who can say they know the U.S. president or an ambassador or even a famous actor or actress feel important. But you and I can say that of the living God. What does that do to you? I hope you never recover! But if you've lost that wonder, simply ask God to give it back—because it's surely the most wondrous thing in all of heaven and earth.

Still, that's not the only thing that happens when you know God.

KNOWING CHRIST DISCIPLE TO TEACHER

The second relationship that opens when you know Jesus and begin to get honest with him is that you become a learner, a student, a disciple. You sit at his elbow and drink in all kinds of wondrous things about God, the universe, love and goodness. You get to sit, like Mary did in Luke 10:38-42, at Jesus' feet to learn from the greatest teacher of all time. You can ask him any question, bring him any concern, debate with him about any dilemma, and he will answer you. He will listen, too, as long as you want to talk. He will guide you to the answers to all kinds of problems and needs as you grow in his love.

Have you ever thought what an amazing thing it is that you have the ear of the living God? Have you sought God to learn all the ins and outs of theology, biblical truth and the wisdom of the Scriptures? Have you taken a question to him and been awed as he revealed the answer to you through study, prayer and others' words?

Martin Luther was once asked what he had to do that day. He replied, "Work, work and more work from early until late. In fact, I have so much to do that I shall spend the first three hours in prayer." With that kind of prayer life, is it any wonder that the person most written about in human history (after Jesus) is Martin Luther?

My friend Teresa Vining has written a powerful book on doubts she had as a Christian, called *Making Your Faith Your Own*. What I most enjoyed about reading it was the way she took me through the same process of discovery she followed as she sought answers to apologetic questions like "Can we trust the Bible?" "What about science?" and "What does God say about the problem of evil and suffering?"

When I told Teresa how much I enjoyed the book, she said something that struck me. "Well, it was just God. He took me through the whole thing to help me get my faith in order." I marveled at that because that is the same thing I have found with God. He is not afraid of any question I throw at him. He doesn't quail in terror because I've unearthed the latest findings of modern science and he hasn't had a chance to read the papers on it yet. He never reels in shock when I fall at his feet and say, "My professor said Jesus was not born of a virgin, but that a Roman soldier and Mary had relations. Is this true?" God doesn't blink when we tell him about our problem with hatred or a vice or an addiction, and he doesn't even condemn us. Rather, he says, "Okay, let's work through this together."

Getting honest with God means learning to give every problem and need to him before we've exhausted all other possibilities. It means involving him in our life at all junctures, not just when all other options have run out. Have you ever thought how incredible that is? People pay counselors thousands of dollars a year for their wisdom on a topic, and many of them are greatly helped, yet we Christians can gain God's ear at the drop of a prayer.

And yet that's just a small part of knowing God intimately.

KNOWING CHRIST FOLLOWER TO LEADER

A third element in our relationship with Christ is that he becomes our Leader, our King, the One whom we can trust to lead and guide us step by step through life. But he is no tyrant, no cruel taskmaster.

As he said in Matthew 11:30, his "yoke is easy" and his "burden is light." He is a master who leads by example, who shows the way by blazing the trail before us. We have a leader who never worries about the future, who forgives the past and who guides us in the present. Getting honest with God through our intimacy with him calls for submission to his leadership and a continual conversational give-and-take about the ways he is leading us. What more could we ask for?

I have read several times of a turning point in American history during the American Revolution. In the winter of 1777-1778 the American army under George Washington wintered at Valley Forge. There, under gray, snowy skies, the soldiers fought for life as many of them faced starvation, disease and exposure. Hundreds died. When Washington received word that the British were marching on Trenton, he tried to rally his troops. Many wouldn't even step out of their huts. Then Washington went to his knees in the snow and called upon his one true Leader for help in leading his men. God answered, his troops rallied and Washington marched those tattered, cold, worn men to their first major victory over the British.

It was a turning point for America. Until then, the cause had looked lost. After that and many other victories, the Americans ended up at Yorktown, where General Cornwallis gave the final surrender of the British forces to Washington. I wonder what might have happened if Washington had not gone to his Leader at that crucial moment at Valley Forge and pled for help?

God doesn't just give us his word. He doesn't simply throw a sheaf of commands at us. He doesn't only fill our mental library with information. He gives us himself.

That is a marvel. But that's not everything.

KNOWING CHRIST FRIEND TO FRIEND

When the disciples walked back with Jesus to where Jesus was staying, they were becoming friends with the Lord. God doesn't just want to answer our questions. He doesn't only want to teach us all his truth. It's not even that he longs to lead us to glory. No, he wants to be friends with us.

Being friends with God doesn't mitigate any of the other elements of our relationship with him as learner, disciple, follower or anything else. But this is one truth that we truly should never recover from: the God of the universe wants to be our Friend. No, not just a friend. An intimate. A sharer in our journey. A partaker in our personality. A rejoicer who rejoices with us and a weeper who weeps with us. One to whom we can tell our deepest secrets.

God is the ultimate Best Friend. He will listen to any complaint and not berate us. He will be there when we need help, no questions asked. He will hang out with us whether we're losers or winners. He will never act ashamed that we're members of his crew. And he will always, always, always stick with us, even when we mess up, even when we sin, even when we totally displease him. He's that kind of Friend.

One of my favorite passages from *The Lion, the Witch and the Wardrobe*—the first book in the wonderful Chronicles of Narnia series by C. S. Lewis—occurs toward the end of the book. There Aslan (the lion who symbolizes Jesus in the series) returns to Narnia to save it from the White Witch. The witch has the power to turn all her enemies into stone with her magic wand. Silent statues stud her castle grounds, all of them Narnians who ended up on the wrong end of her wand.

Aslan takes the two girls in the story, Lucy and Susan, on his back to the witch's castle even as their brothers, Peter and Edmund, battle the White Witch far away. At the castle Aslan hurries through the grounds, breathing on each statue. As he does so, they return to life, including a lion who literally roars back to life.

When all the victims of the White Witch are restored, Aslan announces that they must all rush back to the battle. He tells the slower creatures—fauns, dwarves and so on—to mount the backs of the swifter leopards, giants and lions so they can get to the battle without delay. Then he says, "Those who are good with their noses must come in the front with us lions to smell out where the battle is."

Everyone gets going, but then Lewis writes, "The most pleased of the lot was the other lion, who kept running about everywhere pretending to be very busy but really in order to say to everyone he met, 'Did you hear what he said? *Us lions.* That means him and me. *Us lions.* That's what I like about Aslan. No side, no stand-off-ishness. *Us lions.* That meant him and me.'"

Him and me! What an incredible truth and reality.

One day each of us will stand before Jesus. He will greet us, call us by name and recognize us before the men and women of faith from all time. Perhaps he will say something like "This fine Christian served me during the twenty-first century. He is my friend. Welcome him." Then he will show before billions what we did in our lives to honor and love him.

I honestly think Jesus has that moment planned so that we will be humbled, amazed and overjoyed. It will be our crowning moment of all time, putting to shame anything we might have won in this world—Pulitzers, Nobels, Grammys and Oscars combined. We will never forget the moment when Jesus praises, honors and even exalts us before the whole company of heaven and earth.

One day, in real time, we will stand before Jesus, and his calling us his friends will mean far more than anything else. He will tell the billions of all time that he *knows* us, and they will understand that we are intimate friends who love each other.

What do you want most from God? What desire burns within you, such that you believe you can't live without it? What is it you long for? Isn't it him—unembellished, plain, simple Lord Jesus Christ, Savior of the world, King of creation, Teacher and Leader par excellence, the Friend of friends? Isn't it just to know him as much as it's possible to know him in this world? Isn't it to sit with him and talk and learn and be intimate and share a joke, or maybe a tear, with the one Person who fully understands and cares about us and our lives?

Getting honest with Jesus means getting intimate in those ways with him—seeker to Savior, disciple to Teacher, follower to Leader and friend to Friend. If those are the things you seek, then Jesus says to you: "Come, and you will see."

GETTING HONEST

1. As you go through your day, work at being conscious that Jesus is with you. Thank him at moments when gratitude seems warranted. Praise him for a sight, a feeling or a thought that has come to you. Let him know you love him.

2. Think about the four ways of relating to Jesus. Which is most real to you—seeker to Savior, disciple to Teacher, follower to Leader or friend to Friend?

   Ask him to help you build on that and then to begin to experience the others in all their glory.

2

THE PRAYER IN ANGER
God Knows How to Deal with It

Jonah was greatly displeased and became angry. He prayed to the LORD, "O LORD, is this not what I said when I was still at home? That is why I was so quick to flee to Tarshish. I knew that you are a gracious and compassionate God, slow to anger and abounding in love, a God who relents from sending calamity. Now, O LORD, take away my life, for it is better for me to die than to live."

But the LORD replied, "Have you any right to be angry?"

JONAH 4:1-4

PEOPLE BECOME ANGRY WITH GOD for all sorts of reasons. Something has occurred—a breakup with a love interest, the loss of a job, the birth of a handicapped child—that we believe God somehow caused or certainly didn't prevent. So we become bitter and angry at him because deep down we believe he's responsible. God asks us to do something—become a missionary, witness to a coworker, do a tough job at church—and we don't want to. So we get upset, stonewall God, push him away, refuse to listen. It can be anything. But if we see God as the final Judge and Ruler in all matters, believe God is sovereign over the world, we probably will see any calamity, problem, bad situation or interruption as God's personal responsibility.

What's worse, some Christians spend months or years caterwauling about whatever it is they've been denied, forced to do or have given up. I know. It happened with me and my poetry.

HOLDING GOD RESPONSIBLE

In my last two years of college I developed a powerful interest in writing poetry. I spent hours a day at it, crafting poems like an artist might design a monument. Then during the summer after graduation, just when my fascination with poetry was at a peak, I became a Christian.

In those early Christian days my interest in poetry did not wane. In fact, I spent hours a day writing all kinds of wild and wonderful poems about everything from cockroaches to the majesty of the universe. I found, though, that I couldn't write about God, Jesus or my experience as a Christian—at least not nearly so well as I could write about secular material. I wondered about this, but deep down I believed God wanted me to be a poet, so I wrote like a maniac.

Then one night the Spirit of God seemed to speak to me and tell me I needed to give it up. Poetry had become my god. The notion that I had to burn everything I'd written filled my mind.

I don't know if you've ever had such an experience. In my life, though, several times God has spoken to me in some undeniable, internal way. On this occasion I could not escape it, and I knew I had to take action.

Some people might think God's command to me to burn my poetry was heartless, cruel, not something we would expect of the Lord God. But more than once in biblical times God required someone to do something he or she did not want to do. When he called Moses to go back to the Israelites and lead them out of slavery, Moses wanted nothing to do with it and argued with God vociferously about finding someone else. David fought his own battle with God over his sin with Bathsheba. Though little is said of the time between his sin and Nathan's confrontation, I'm sure David fought God off many times as the Lord tried to speak to him about the situation. Jesus in Gethsemane sought release from his work on the cross. Even though he submitted to God's will at the end, he still sweat drops of blood during the discussion. And Peter, while on a rooftop, argued with God about giving up his old life as a food-Pharisee (eating only foods approved in the laws of Israel) and turning to the new open and free way of Christ.

While God is generally loving and gentle, he can also be firm and direct, like he was about my poetry. I battled for several days, arguing that I would only write Christian material and I would only do it to glorify him. But none of it held. "Burn it," he seemed to say with a finality that sounded like a death knell. Getting honest with God sometimes means getting honest about something he feels he must take away from us.

After all the arguments about my poetry, I gathered up the pages with a heavy heart and marched to the fireplace in the ski lodge where I worked. In only minutes I had fed all my material to the flames. Some of my friends and coworkers walked by and asked what I was doing. I explained. Several thought I was nuts—they knew of my love for the eloquent word. "Why are you doing this? What's wrong? This is years of work!"

I had no answer. They wouldn't understand. They weren't Christians.

The deed done, I felt saddened—but also energized, because I believed I had followed God's will. The anger came a few days after all the poems had gone up in smoke. What had I done? What had God made me do? Why? I felt I had destroyed my dream of becoming a prizewinning poet, and God had *made me do it*.

I fumed and fussed and froze out God for some time in my anguish and anger over what I had now begun to think may have been the demand of a legalistic potentate. God was mean. God was cruel. God didn't understand.

While I fretted about all this, what did God do? Oh, occasionally he'd whisper, "Do you really think I meant that?" or "Do you really believe this is the way it is?" or "How can you say that with all the other blessings you have?"

I forced it all out of my head. I grumbled for weeks. But then I started to simmer down and see that maybe I'd let my poetry take too big a slot in my life and schedule. At that point God said to me, "Now you're ready to write. Go to it."

I was astonished. "You want me to write?"

"I gave you talent. Don't you expect me to tell you to use it?"

"But you took everything away."

"And now I'm giving it all back. All of that poetry is still in your head and heart. You just needed a correction, is all."

I soon found that the talent and desire still existed, and the words were more beautiful than before. This is one of the poems that came out of that time:

Birth at Bethlehem

Strange:
from a dappled blue egg,
a fragile crack, a yellow beak,
and then the chirping hungry jaw
of a robin.

Even stranger:
upon the crisp straw, the wet,
struggling form of a filly
nuzzling the mare's warm nipple.

Stranger still: The jagged screech of a child,
tiny fingers grasping a breast,
tiny blue eyes meeting
a mother's misty browns
and locking on.

Strangest of all:
from the untried womb of a virgin:
the iron thunder and bright lightning
of heaven: the pink body of God
trembling gently in a feed trough.

Strange? No.
Wonderful!
Marvelous!
Astonishing!

       Holy.

Nonetheless I regretted vilifying God and yelling at him about him taking away everything important to me. What a waste of time and energy!

God said to me, "Nothing is wasted. I use it all for good. You have grown. And I can now bless you because your poetry's not an idol."

I've found that for all of us there are moments when God forces himself upon us in a way that we try to fight. But ultimately, if we're really walking with him, we submit. C. S. Lewis talked about how he was dragged "kicking and screaming into the kingdom of God." I've read of other men—Charles Spurgeon, Martin Luther, Martin Luther King Jr.—facing a transformational moment in their lives that they knew God called them to but that they shrank from with all their hearts. In some cases they became angry and even resentful until they saw the glory behind the call.

With that in mind, let's ask: Is it ever okay to get angry at God? To slam doors and stomp? To cut loose with a swearword or two?

IS IT EVER OKAY?

Getting honest with God means getting honest with him about our anger. About our anger directed at him. About the anger that festers deep inside for days, possibly years, over something we've locked deep down in our soul as if to conceal it from God.

If a mild-mannered person gets angry at his or her spouse, kids, relatives, friends or coworkers, you can be sure that person has been angry at God. It could be a seething, verbal anger that he releases only when he knows he's absolutely alone. Or it might be an argumentative, complaining anger that comes out in bitterness and general unhappiness with the life God has given her.

Whatever way we manifest it, if we look hard enough, we will probably find occasions when we've been royally ripped at God.

Cain was. After God rejected his sacrifice and commended Abel's, his anger shot out in an act of murder.

Moses let it roar on occasion. At one point when Israel complained bitterly to Moses about God's treatment of them in the wilderness, Moses flamed so sharply that his anger brought God's immediate denunciation and a searing punishment: he was forbidden to ever enter the Promised Land with the people he'd led for forty years.

Job, Samson, Samuel, King Saul, King David and most of the prophets exhibited anger, often directed at God the Father.

In the New Testament, Paul was an angry young man before his conversion, helping to murder Christians because he hated them. Do you think that anger just disappeared because he became a believer?

And then there are James and John, the "sons of thunder." Can't you see them exploding over something they disliked?

One of my friends went through a terrible time of anger at God over the birth of a severely handicapped daughter. At times, Alsie told me, she had to go into her bedroom and scream at God because her anger became so fierce. At moments like that, she half expected God to incinerate her on the spot. She told me, "I was sure my husband would come home and find a soot-blackened patch on the carpet where I last stood."

Does being a godly Christian automatically eliminate our propensity to get angry at God? Certainly not, though there is righteous anger and there is unrighteous anger.

The story of Jonah is the classic case of unrighteous anger leveled at God. This prophet disagreed so much with God's orders that at one point he requested that God kill him rather than let him see God's grace given to the enemy. Yet through Jonah God painted a marvelous picture of how he deals with us when we're angry. If Jonah is any indication, we are confronted with a God of infinite grace and patience. What exactly does Jonah show us?

THE CLASSIC CASE

If you're rusty on the story of Jonah, read the book. It's short, though not so sweet.

A great enemy lurked on Israel's horizon. Assyria ranks as one of the most ruthless empires ever to exist on earth. Its epicenter was the city of Nineveh, one of the great cities of antiquity. Towering walls circled the city, protecting it from enemies.

Jonah lived and prophesied in the northern kingdom of Israel during the reign of Jeroboam II, around 760 B.C. At the time, Assyria had conquered much of the Middle Eastern world. Israel feared this cruel giant, whose captains were known to publicly skin alive the leaders of each city they captured.

One day God commanded Jonah to travel nearly five hundred miles from his homeland to warn Nineveh of impending doom. God had seen the people's wickedness and wanted Jonah to warn them that in forty days God would destroy their city.

Jonah balked at such a mission. *Help the enemies of my people?* he probably thought. *Give them a chance to repent? No way.*

Jonah hurried to the nearest port, found a ship headed for Tarshish, located on the coast of Spain—in the opposite direction of Nineveh. He climbed down into the hold of the ship and fell into a deep asleep. Soon after the ship left Joppa, a port on the western coast of Israel, God hurled a storm on the sea specifically to stop Jonah.

This reveals a first principle of how to get honest with God when we're angry at him. God let Jonah vent his anger, but he also protected Jonah from going too far afield with his self-defeating impulses.

Notice what happened: Jonah ran from God. He wanted nothing to do with God's mission. God could have stopped Jonah just as he halted Balaam, when the donkey spoke to his master about an angel in his path. He could have spoken to him like he did with Paul on the road to Damascus, when Jesus appeared in an explosion of light and confronted the soon-to-be apostle. But in this case God did nothing. He let Jonah leave Israel and made no effort to stop him until he was at sea.

When we begin to get honest with God about our anger, we may run many miles from him. God has purposefully let us go to mull over our anger. He does not force us to do his will but gives us a chance to douse the teeming cauldron in our souls with a hike into the wilderness.

The interesting thing is that Jonah ran. Why didn't he just say, "I won't do it"? Why didn't Jonah ignore God and prune his fig tree (or whatever was in his garden)? Or say, "Just leave me alone"? I think there's a simple reason. When you're angry at that level, you don't think clearly. Perhaps Jonah had experienced God's pressure before. Maybe he thought that if he could just get on a ship going somewhere else, God would give up. "Okay, you win, Jonah. Have a nice vacation."

But perhaps something else was happening here. Jonah wanted to do something to show God just how upset he was about this mission. To ignore God or refuse wasn't enough. Jonah had to tell God off a little. He wanted to do something that showed God he was wrong about trying to help Nineveh. Jonah had to shove it in God's face. "You think you can do this to me? Well, take that!" So he ran.

I've seen people like that. They're so enraged that you can't reason with them. They don't want discussion; they want their way. At times, I know, I've been so angry at God that I just didn't want to hear anything from him (or my wife or kids) about it. God probably said, "Let it run its course. He'll be wrung out soon enough."

The God who lets us vent, the Lord who lets us run when we're upset, is a God far more worthy of worship than a god who would squash us like a bug if we talked out of turn at him.

I once had a friend whose father was an ill-tempered person who never let anyone say a contrary word. His family lived in fear of his moods. They watched every syllable that came out of their mouths, afraid he'd slap them silly for voicing dissent or offering a well-reasoned opinion. Such people are impossible to get along with. Yet I know many Christians who make God out to be precisely that kind of mean-spirited ogre who can't deal with us voicing a complaint. They live in fear that God will destroy their lives if they ever speak what they really feel. Nonetheless, if we can't get honest with God about our anger, what can we get honest about? People who hide such anger often reap a whirlwind of unsettling emotions and pangs, including depression, anxiety and abject fear.

The God who lets us feel our anger is a majestic God who truly understands human nature. God let Jonah run because he is wise and understanding and because he knows what will and won't work. God had to let Jonah run, for only through giving him that freedom could Jonah ever learn anything. We sometimes have to give people the opportunity to come to their senses. I think this was what God was doing with Jonah. Getting honest with God sometimes means God gets honest with us and lets us run off our steam until we run out of steam.

THE STORM

To be sure, God will let us rush off to places unknown in our anger. But he will not stand by and let us destroy his plan or ourselves. So when Jonah ran off, God immediately acted.

While Jonah lay in the hold fast asleep, God sent such a fierce storm that the sailors were soon throwing their cargo into the waves to lighten their load and save the ship. The crew called on their gods for mercy, but that did no good. So as they hurried down into the hold to cast more goods overboard, they found Jonah, asleep. The storm hadn't even roused him.

Immediately the captain told Jonah to call on his God about the storm. Maybe Jonah's God would hear, since the sailors' gods didn't seem to. This captain just wanted to cover all the bases.

Still the storm raged. So the captain decided to use a common method to pinpoint the real culprit. He cast lots, and the lot fell on Jonah. The sailors immediately asked him who he was and where he was from and what he knew about the storm. Jonah revealed that he was a Hebrew and feared the living and true God. He also told them he was running from God because he didn't want to go on a mission God had called him to.

Undoubtedly the sailors turned hot pink with rage. They all knew about the God of the Hebrews—how he occasionally wiped out whole countries for hurting Israel. The Hebrews' God definitely could be hot-blooded in certain situations.

Thus the captain couldn't believe his ears. "How could you do this?" he asked. They'd lost all their cargo and were in danger of losing the ship and their lives. All of this because Jonah had defied this God?

Absolutely. While God will let you run, he will not let you off the hook about doing the right thing. So God shamed Jonah before the whole crew.

Nonetheless Jonah didn't budge. He was so angry at God that he told the sailors to cast him overboard and let him drown. Then the storm would stop.

Have you ever been there? You're so mad at God that you'd prefer dying to giving in and admitting that God is right and you are wrong.

There have been times when I have let blissful thoughts of a sorrowful death course through my mind when I didn't like what God was doing in my life. What was I really doing? I wanted to get back at God. I wanted to hurt him like I felt he'd hurt me. So instead of thinking realistically, I would conjure up pictures in my head of me dying a terrible death. I would see all my family, friends and neighbors weeping and shouting recriminations over how badly I had been treated.

It's complete foolishness. But that was what Jonah was doing. He was so angry that he would rather die than obey God. Think about it: Wasn't there another option? Couldn't Jonah have said to the sailors, "I've been running away from God. But just put me off at the nearest port and I'll continue doing what God wants"? I'm sure the storm would have stopped then and there. But Jonah wasn't going to give God an inch. So he told the sailors to throw him overboard.

The sailors refused. They didn't want God mad at them, too, for killing his prophet. So they rowed desperately for land.

The storm got worse. It was hopeless. The sailors looked at Jonah one more time; he gestured to the side of the boat; and they finally gave in, imploring God not to hold Jonah's death against them. Then they dumped Jonah overboard.

Immediately the storm stopped. The whole crew fell to their knees and worshiped the living and true God. They were Jonah's first real converts. Meanwhile, Jonah and his miserable little gripe sank into the depths.

Think about this. God gave Jonah several opportunities to repent. One, before he left for Joppa. Two, when the captain found him in the hold. Three, when the lots were cast. And four, when the crew refused to throw him overboard. How many chances did this guy need before he'd repent? Apparently, many. Amazingly, though, God was willing to give Jonah those chances.

Have you ever wondered just how much anger and rebellion God will put up with? How insolent can you be before God destroys you?

God gives us a very long leash in letting us tell him off! Theodore Roethke, the famed poet, wrote in "The Decision" that "running from God's the longest race of all." Jonah was learning that. He could run, but he couldn't hide.

Here the grim saga of Jonah's merry temper tantrum took another twist. He sank so deeply into the sea that he actually touched seaweed. At that point Jonah received a wake-up call.

Wait a second! I'm about to die. I'm going to face God with all this sinful anger behind me, and I may just be cast into hell for all eternity. These must have been the thoughts in Jonah's mind. So Jonah did the first thing that came to mind under such circumstances. He cried out, "Save me, Lord!"

You would think God might say, "Serves you right. Die the death of the wicked, you reprobate!" But he didn't. He heard Jonah's prayer from the depths of the sea and he sent a giant fish to swallow him. The second chapter of the book of Jonah is Jonah's thanksgiving song to God for saving him. He prayed it while inside the fish's belly.

Now get this: Jonah said nothing in this prayer about being willing to go to Nineveh. He said nothing about repentance and a willingness to help save the Ninevites. He only said, "What I have vowed I will make good" (Jonah 2:9). That could simply mean he intended to go to the temple and make the proper sacrifices for his sin and thanksgiving.

The fish vomited Jonah on the beach and God told Jonah a second time, "Go to Nineveh." Nothing had changed. It was the same mission. Jonah had simply wasted his time and God's time, nearly destroyed a ship and its crew, and caused himself to smell like the inside of a fish's stomach.

But Jonah had partially learned his lesson. He would not run again. No, he saw the futility of that. So he went along with God. Somewhat.

THE REVIVAL

Jonah marched to Nineveh and preached, and the whole city repented, hoping God would not destroy them if they showed faith and confessed their sins. Jonah was the catalyst for perhaps the greatest revival in the history of the world, in which thousands, and possibly millions, of souls became believers in Jehovah. Jonah had never seen anything like this in his homeland. In fact Israel was so wicked that God would soon have Assyria destroy the nation and carry them all into slavery.

Wasn't this something Jonah could rejoice in? Isn't saving souls the passion of a prophet? Isn't revival what prophets like Elijah and Elisha longed for and never participated in? Jonah's experience was the dream of every preacher in history. Revival! The powerful work of God. The finger of God on the pulse of a nation.

But this isn't what Jonah wanted. Revival in Israel? Sure, bring it on. But for the enemies of Israel? For my personal enemies? "Forget it! I'd rather die than see that happen," Jonah said.

Jonah was now even angrier than he had been earlier. Why? Because this was the very reason he ran. He didn't want God to have mercy on the Ninevites and pardon them. Jonah trekked out to a hill overlooking the city and watched with angry eyes and a mind reeling with hate, demanding that God destroy the city anyway.

Isn't this astonishing? Jonah couldn't find a sliver of happiness in his heart. He couldn't see any good in this event. He would have preferred that the Ninevites all die rather than that any become committed disciples who might, because of their faith, actually become supporters of Israel instead of enemies.

Jonah told God, "O LORD, is this not what I said when I was still at home? . . . I knew that you are a gracious and compassionate God, slow to anger and abounding in love, a God who relents from

sending calamity. Now, O LORD, take away my life, for it is better
for me to die than to live" (Jonah 4:2-3).

Have you ever resented it when a criminal becomes a Christian
and starts shouting about how great God is? Have you ever become
a little upset when a black sheep in your family finally comes to
Christ and gets blessed while you experience joyless faith minus
such blessings? I remember times meeting new Christians who
seemed to be having a banquet of abundant life in their newfound
faith. Occasionally I resented their joy because at the time I had
none myself.

We can become angry about the most trivial things. And yet that
anger is real, it's hurtful and it's devastating. Getting honest with God
means admitting the anger, admitting the sin behind it and moving
on with a new desire to please him and walk in his will.

Unfortunately Jonah still didn't feel that way. He sat on the hill and
saw the Ninevites whooping it up because God had relented. Undoubtedly he felt they didn't deserve this grace. He believed they
were enemies and they should be destroyed. "No," went Jonah's man-
tra, "they should burn."

But that's what happens when we're angry at God. We can't enjoy
anything, even having God majestically work through us. Instead we
feel angrier. We harbor a sense of betrayal. We believe God has really
let us down.

THE TEACHER VISITS

As Jonah sat on the hill, God did something amazing: he made a
gourd plant grow over Jonah, providing him with an on-site air con-
ditioning unit. Jonah lay in the shade, overwhelmed with God's
goodness. He drank in the atmosphere, thinking, *Well, finally God is
doing something right.*

But God had more in mind than cooling Jonah, so he sent a worm that killed the plant. He followed that with a scorching wind.

Jonah got mad again.

For the fourth time in the book, God spoke gently to Jonah. "Do you have a right to be angry about the vine?" (Jonah 4:9).

Jonah responded, "I do. I am angry enough to die" (Jonah 4:9).

God made his final pitch, the lesson he wanted to drive home in this scenario. "You have been concerned about this vine, though you did not tend it or make it grow. It sprang up overnight and died overnight. But Nineveh has more than a hundred and twenty thousand people who cannot tell their right hand from their left. . . . Should I not be concerned about that great city?" (Jonah 4:10-11).

The book ends on that question. Most scholars believe Jonah learned his lesson—that's why, they think, he wrote the book. What was that lesson? To care about lost people everywhere, even if they are also your enemies.

I read the book of Jonah and I marvel at God's patience with this prophet. Why did God hang in there with this nasty man and his ugly attitude? I think there's one reason: because God doesn't consider any believer not worth the trouble. Or to put it positively: God cares so much about every believer that he'll give them extra chances and go to much trouble to help them learn the truth.

Have you ever felt that loving some people is just not worth the trouble? Have you ever acted kindly toward someone, only to be treated badly? Mark Twain once said, "A dog won't bite the hand that feeds it. This is the principal difference between a dog and a man." I have frequently seen people bite the hands that fed them. I have been bitten, and, shamefully, I have bitten others. Most people are not patient about such treatment.

But what happens when we're angry at God? How do we get hon-

est with him, and he with us? We talk it out. We vent, if necessary.
We let him know how we feel. If we need time, he gives us time to
think, to work through our feelings, to yell.

What happens when we curse God and feel he has mistreated us?
What happens when we give him the silent treatment, when we run
off into sin to get back at him? Again, he teaches us to get honest. He
is patient with us. He bides his time. As with Jonah, he doesn't push
us or "God-handle" us, but he finds the right moment to teach the
great lesson we need to learn, and then he leaves it to us to apply it.

What happens when we really run from God, and we mess up our
lives with sin and debauchery and all the wrong choices? What happens when our anger controls us so much that we destroy ourselves,
thinking this will cause God heartache? He works with us, woos us,
lets us vent, draws us back to himself and never gives up on us. Did
you hear that? He *never gives up on us.*

That's incredible. When I consider how many people I've given up
on—members of my family, children who have rebelled, friends and
relatives who skirt around the subject of Christ—I know we have a
God who can be trusted to stick with the job until it's done. No
amount of anger, bitterness, dejection, disappointment or discouragement on our part throws him. He remains compassionate, contin-
ually wooing us until the light dawns in our hearts and we embrace
the truth.

THE INCLINED EAR

I read of a missionary who was trying to translate Psalm 40 into the
native language of a tribe. He came upon "I waited patiently for the
LORD; And he inclined to me, and heard my cry" (Psalm 40:1 NASB).
He knew of no word in the tribe's language that pictured the word
"inclined." He asked God to show him the right wording.

One day he saw a village grandfather with his grandson on his knee. The boy had turned his face up to the grandfather to speak, and the grandfather tilted his head so his ear was close to the boy's lips. The missionary ran over to the old man, asking him what he was doing. The grandfather said, "I am spreading my ear out like a blanket."

So the missionary ran home and translated Psalm 40, "I waited patiently for the Lord, and he spread out his ear like a blanket and heard my cry" (*Our Daily Bread*).

What an apt image of God's stance with us when we are angry! God does not want us to be afraid to tell him how we really feel. He does not slap us down for voicing complaints, frustration or even deep anger. No, God spreads his ear like a blanket and lets us give him an earful, if that is what we need to do at the moment. This does not mean he will agree with us, or even change his plan because of our anger, but it does mean we have a heavenly Father who will always listen and not condemn and who will patiently let us spill our venom until he can move us into circumstances in which we'll listen to him.

Getting honest with him releases us not only to speak truth but also to trust and to love God as he most desires. He will never turn a deaf ear to us when we cry out in anger, because he loves us enough to let us be truly ourselves. That's a God I can worship with abandon.

GETTING HONEST

1. Think of the last time you were angry with God. How did you handle it?

2. What would you like to change about how you handle anger at God?

3. Take the time today to tell God what's truly on your heart, whether it's something you're angry about or just something you need to get out. Make this a practice every day. In time you will learn to hold nothing back from God. That will deepen your relationship with him like nothing else.

3

THE PRAYER OF RELINQUISHMENT
Surrender All to God

Whenever Hannah went up to the house of the LORD, her rival provoked her till she wept and would not eat. Elkanah her husband would say to her, "Hannah, why are you weeping? Why don't you eat? Why are you downhearted? Don't I mean more to you than ten sons?"

Once when they had finished eating and drinking in Shiloh, Hannah stood up. Now Eli the priest was sitting on a chair by the doorpost of the LORD's temple. In bitterness of soul Hannah wept much and prayed to the LORD. And she made a vow, saying, "O LORD Almighty, if you will only look upon your servant's misery and remember me, and not forget your servant but give her a son, then I will give him to the LORD for all the days of his life, and no razor will ever be used on his head."

1 SAMUEL 1:7-11

ONE OF THE STRONGEST HUMAN TENDENCIES is that of wanting to hang on to what is most precious to us. This is true in an earthly sense. We love our children; we safeguard them with bike helmets and seat belts and instructions to beware of strangers. We love our cars; we install alarm systems in them so that no one will steal them. We love our financial nest eggs; we scheme endlessly to come up with the best way of keeping our money safe and making it grow.

The same is true in a spiritual sense. Oh, we may sing hymns and choruses about surrendering all to God, but "surrendering" sounds all too much like "losing" when it comes to what we really care about. How about that pet sin? Ready to give that up? How about that dream you keep striving to make a reality? What if God has other plans for you? The rich young ruler who encountered Jesus obeyed every commandment but wasn't prepared to give up his wealth. Can you relate to him? If we are really going to "seek first his kingdom and his righteousness" (Matthew 6:33), then we have to be ready to tell God (and mean it), "You can have everything. All I want is you!"

The spiritual struggle over relinquishing all we have and are to the Lord is largely played out in our prayer life. Certainly that was true for one of the greatest believers in Scripture: a woman named Hannah. She learned how to get honest with God about something she dearly wanted.

Meet Hannah

We meet Hannah only once in Scripture, in the opening chapters of 1 Samuel. There we learn a number of basic facts about Hannah. The first wife of a godly man named Elkanah, she was barren and didn't have children. Elkanah's second wife, Peninnah, bore several children rather quickly and made Hannah's life miserable with taunts, mocking and scorn over the fact that Hannah had no children. Furthermore, we learn that Elkanah took his family to the worship center in Shiloh every year and made the prescribed sacrifices. But he always gave a double sacrifice for Hannah, asking God to give her children. Each year when she didn't conceive, Hannah sank into a miserable state of depression.

Whenever I find out what people really want, I soon discover one of two things: what they want is almost ridiculously trivial ("All I want is that time-share in Branson") or else it's only one of a long line of things that grow ever larger with time (first it's a good day at the beach, then it's a vacation to Hawaii, later it's a chateau in Switzerland). Some people, Christians included, are bottomless pits of wants.

But every now and then you meet a person like Hannah, who really had only one desire. She had a husband who loved her and a decent home life—she wasn't homeless or poor. She voiced no major complaints. She probably knew she should focus on what she did have rather than what she didn't have. But there was this one thing . . .

That first year she didn't get pregnant, she probably thought, *Oh well, it doesn't always happen right away.* Through the second year, Hannah most likely began to feel nervous. Was something wrong? She may have consulted with the doctors, talked to the priest. They might have mixed their potions or prayed and hoped for the best. Nothing happened.

Elkanah, though, wanted children. So, being practical, he married a second woman. She wasn't nearly as nice as Hannah, but she immediately broke all records for bearing children. This feat, however, didn't win Elkanah's total absorption. He tried to be equally loving with each wife. But for Peninnah, that wasn't enough. So she made Hannah's life torture. After all, wasn't she the one who had borne Elkanah the heir?

A barren woman in Israel wore the ultimate scarlet letter of shame. Today we might argue that a woman does not need children for fulfillment; she can find completion in marriage, a career, extended family and so on. But in Hannah's day a woman's primary function, aspiration and goal was to be a mother. No matter what your station in life, if you had children, you were truly blessed.

Barrenness signified not only incompetence and personal failure but also God's displeasure. Only God could open the womb, the Jews believed, and if God had closed it, you could be sure he had strong reasons. Sin was a primary reason, people thought, but perhaps other things, like having the wrong lineage or marrying outside Israel, could account for barrenness too. Whatever the reasons, barrenness turned into a sign of shame you wore on your cloak every day for all your life.

Hannah, though, being a woman of faith, probably knew about her ancestors Sarah, Rebekah and Rachel, each of whom had a child only after a period of barrenness. Like them, she began to solicit heaven with sacrifices and prayer. Yet it got her nowhere.

By now probably well into her thirties, she was becoming despondent. She peered out the window while cleaning and spied children playing in the dirt. Despair flooded her soul, reminding her they weren't her children; they belonged to another, a woman who was blessed by God. As she walked down the street, stepping out of the way of playing teens, the depression streamed over her again. *Why am I the only one in town who doesn't have children? What have I done wrong?*

Undoubtedly Hannah asked those questions over and over. But she could find no answers. She scoured her soul, her day and her year, searching for foul deeds, harsh words or errant thoughts. But she could find no sin worthy of this disgrace. So she begged her husband to sleep with her, while her rival, Peninnah, drummed her fingers on the tabletop, shouting, "When do I get my time with my husband?"

As her mid-thirties loomed before her, the ticking of Hannah's internal clock began to sound like explosions of dynamite. It would soon be too late to have a child, and she knew she couldn't expect the kind of miracles that happened with Sarah, Rebekah and Rachel to happen to her.

During this time of desperation and depression, a change occurred in Hannah's thinking and attitude. She and her husband had tried offering God plenty of the best sacrifices. But that apparently wasn't all God wanted in her case. She may have wished she could bribe God with wealth or some action on her part. But that's not what he was looking for. It was then that she had a startling idea: What if she was willing to give up to the Lord *the very thing that she most wanted?* What if she was willing to give him the son she had for years been praying for on her knees with fasting and much weeping?

The Scriptures gave her this revolutionary idea, for it is the Scriptures that describe the Nazirite vow (Numbers 6:1-21). A Nazirite was a man specially devoted to God. He never cut his hair, never drank wine and could never be around dead people. Samson was a Nazirite. So was John the Baptist. Some say Jesus might have been one. It was a rarity.

In the case of Hannah's future son, she would dedicate the boy to

God even more specially. He would serve God in the worship center every day for the rest of his life, beginning shortly after he was weaned at three or four years old. If God would give her a son, Hannah would give him back to God.

WHAT HANNAH WAS REALLY OFFERING

As we look at Hannah's situation, we see much more than a deal in which she was promising to give God such-and-such if he would grant her wish. No, that sounds like a used-car salesman who agrees to come down two hundred dollars because the kid's fresh out of college. We need to look at what Hannah was really talking about.

Hannah was offering all she had. Having a son was her dream. To give him away at the age of three or four would rip her heart out. And knowing what kind of life he would live as a Nazirite—trying to serve God among so many arrogant, sinful Israelites—could easily make her worry and fear for his life. And Hannah was making an irrevocable decision; once she gave him to the Lord, she could never get him back. And once her son became a Nazirite, her life as his mother ended. Yes, she'd see him now and then, but she wouldn't raise him, wouldn't share those fragrant early years with him, wouldn't witness every transitional stage as he moved from child toward mature man.

My son is now five. I have been party to many of his most crazy, exciting and endearing moments. One day last year, at Christmas time, we were in the car listening to the Chipmunks sing Christmas songs. When I turned the tape player off, my son, Gardner, said, "I want to listen to the chick punks again."

I laughed and said, "Chick punks? Who's that? Madonna and Cher?"

He said, "No, the chick punks—Alvin, Theo-score and Dimon."

I can see scenes from my daughters' lives when they were four, seven, ten, twelve, all the way up to eighteen. I would write down anecdotes about funny and touching things they said and file them for ready reference. We have photo albums full of their pictures as they grew.

I wouldn't miss any of it. Would you trade the right to watch your child grow up just for the privilege of giving birth to him or her?

Hannah was willing to give up all of that just to have a son. Just to give birth to him and cuddle him for a few years. Just to have the experience and the badge of honor of being a mother. The thought of giving that boy up must have torn her to pieces, but she would do it, if God would just let her bring him into the world.

She didn't even ask for other children. She didn't ask God to let her live near the tabernacle where her son would grow up. She could give all that up in exchange for the privilege of bearing him. It was an awesome act of courage, submission and faith.

That year Hannah traveled once again to the tabernacle and talked to God about her proposition. Eli, watching her weep and moan as she prayed the most painful prayer of her life, thought she was drunk. When he confronted her and discovered she was sincere, he asked God to bless her.

God did. The next year Hannah gave birth to Samuel. He would become one of the greatest judges in Israel's history.

Hannah took care of Samuel the best way she knew how in his baby days. No doubt she treasured every one of those days she got to spend with the little fulfillment of her dream. But she did not let her love for the boy shake her determination to carry through on her vow. She kept him only as long as necessary to see that he was started out in life in good health.

After he was weaned, she took the boy with her, young as he was, along with a three-year-old bull, an ephah of flour and a skin of wine, and brought him to the house of the LORD at Shiloh. When they had slaughtered the bull, they brought the boy to Eli, and she said to him, "As surely as you live, my lord, I am the woman who stood here beside you praying to the LORD. I prayed for this child, and the LORD has granted me what I asked of him. So now I give him to the LORD. For his whole life he will be given over to the LORD." And he worshiped the LORD there. (1 Samuel 1:24-28)

How could she follow through on this so easily?

I believe that Hannah, after her "drunken" prayer in the temple, had reached such a level in her love for God that she would have been okay without having a son. Maybe by then she had attained such contentment that she could have accepted her condition.

WHAT DO YOU WANT?

I think that, many times in life, the thing we want is not what we really need. God in his wisdom gives us the blessing he knows will fulfill us. The fact that God did not give us what we originally wanted is forgotten in the joy of the true blessing God has given.

God's blessing comes in many forms. Sometimes it's not what we expect. But what he gives turns out to be what we longed for all along.

God did grant Hannah her request. Why? Had she made him the classic offer he couldn't refuse? Had her pain and distress so touched his heart that he had to help her?

We may never know the answer. We know that God is compassionate and gracious. We know he delights to give his children what they need and desire. We know his heart is that of a giving father who would never withhold good gifts from his children. Jesus himself said God is not like an unkind father who would give his children a stone when they asked for a loaf of bread (Matthew 7:9).

But maybe *Why* is the wrong question. God is good. He loves to give good gifts to all his children. Like a wealthy, happy father, he promises that if we delight in him, he will give us the desires of our heart (Psalm 37:4). Why, then, is it remarkable that God answered Hannah's request? What is befuddling is why he made her wait so long!

I think there are at least two reasons. First, he was waiting for her to reach the point of relinquishment. She probably would not have given her child to God at twenty or twenty-five years old. Maybe she had to go through all the agony to reach that point. After all, if she had other sons and daughters years earlier, what would have been the point then? She would not even have imagined it. God possibly let her to go through that pain so she could become willing to give up Samuel as a Nazirite. I believe God often works this way. He withholds a lesser blessing in order to impart a greater blessing.

But I think there is another, more important reason why God granted Hannah's request at that time. She had to become a certain kind of person in order to make this decision, and it took her a long time to get there. In other words, for her to gain God's blessing she had to grow in character. God had to build her so that through that character she would offer Samuel. God could not simply infuse character into her. Character is something nurtured and developed over long periods of time and growth. Through her pains Hannah grew into the kind of person God wanted her to be all along.

Think of the changes built into Hannah's life as a result of her being denied a son:

Her prayer life became more fervent and passionate. Usually the greatest prayer warriors are those who have been through the battle. Undoubtedly Hannah's battle scars had turned her into quite a woman of prayer.

She learned patience and other virtues through being denied. How do we learn something like patience? By having to be patient. By being put into circumstances that stretch a person's boundaries and teach him or her to be patient.

She discovered the power of perseverance. People who get what they want right away often do not appreciate what they've received. But those who have worked, persevered and been pushed to the limits experience a deeper joy and higher love than those who haven't.

She became dependent on God. Toward the end of her trial, Hannah knew her only hope was in God. Would she have felt that way if she'd turned up pregnant five days after the honeymoon? Dependence is a learned quality. Many find it easy to make their own way and carve out their own success through hard work. Yet those who understand that everything they have—intelligence, talent, ability, determination—is really God's gift will go far with God. You don't discover how much you need God until you *really* need him. Then, when he answers in a powerful way, you know that answer was God's doing. No other kind of answer could be as joyful.

Finally, Hannah became a woman of God. How many times have I heard young people say they want to be men and women of God? But do they realize what they will have to go through to get there? Hannah's experiences turned her into a person far greater and more beautiful in God's eyes than she would ever have become otherwise. She could only become who she would become by enduring that pain and suffering.

Do you see that Hannah's offer was no ordinary offer? This was the passion of a woman who had grown to be a towering spiritual figure. This was the end of a conversation that had started years before as Hannah learned to get honest with God. She finally reached a point at which she was ready to lay everything at God's feet.

In the end God could not resist granting this spiritual giant a giant answer to her prayer.

My Relinquishment

One of the most difficult problems for me as a young Christian was the classic issue of wondering what I was supposed to do with my life. Some people just seem to know. They want to be doctors or lawyers or teachers or architects. But I didn't know what I wanted to be, or what I was supposed to be, while my friends seemed to know.

More important, I didn't want to waste my life doing something I *had* to do just to get by. My mother used to tell me about people who had "settled" on a job or a mate. They couldn't find the one they dreamed about, so they "settled" for something inferior. In the end they didn't lead happy lives.

I remember hearing Billy Graham tell about a time he asked a young man, "What is your fear?" The young man answered, "I'm afraid I'll waste my life." That was my worry. What if I missed God's plan? What if I refused when he called? I was afraid that would happen to me. I would go through life doing jobs I hated and settle for the mediocre rather than find the extraordinary.

As I tried to come to grips with God's will for my life, I thought at first that he must want me to be a doctor, because that was what I had prepared for in college. I talked to him about it many times and even tried to negotiate a bit. "Lord, if I become a doctor, will you still let me write poetry and stories?"

I say that because my real dream was to be a poet, a writer and possibly a college English teacher. I had talked to God about this, but all my profs discouraged me from teaching English; the field was then crowded with candidates. Being a poet, though, was nutcracker crazy. Rarely can anyone make a living from writing poetry. Most writers have to work a "regular" job before they ever reach the point of supporting themselves with writing.

Because of my zeal for Christ, though, quite a few people suggested

I consider training for the ministry. "The ministry?" I replied. "No way." The only ministers I had ever known, before I became a Christian, were short, fat, bald and boring. I didn't want to be identified with them!

That was when God zapped me.

I had graduated from college and taken the year off. One weekend, while working as a ski bum in Vermont, I became depressed. I knew I had to make decisions about my future and couldn't seem to focus on anything I really wanted to go after. I had been talking to God about it for months, and he hadn't answered. Finally I knew I had to have an answer from the Lord. I hurried to a little chapel to complain to God. I didn't like not knowing what I was supposed to do after the winter was over. I told God that as I sat down alone in a pew.

A few minutes later, the still, small voice spoke inside my head: "I want you to go into the ministry!"

I was astonished. The ministry? How could I ever do that?

The voice spoke again, a bit more forcefully. "I want you to go to seminary and become a minister."

This time I spoke out loud: "No way. I can't go into the ministry. I don't know how to do that."

The voice responded, "I want you to train for the ministry."

"I can't be a minister," I said with genuine fear. "I don't know how to speak in public. I'm terrified of it." That was a serious problem. I had never been able to speak in front of a group. My heart always pounded, my forehead sweat and I felt like vomiting. I knew I couldn't face that.

We went back and forth. In the end, though, I couldn't keep fighting. So I said, "All right, I'll be a minister on certain conditions. You have to do four things first. First of all, you'll have to show me that I can speak in public. Second, you'll have to show me I can lead people to Christ." (I'd never led anyone to the Lord at that point, and before I'd become a Christian, I may have even led a few away from him!) "Third," I said, "you'll have to show me I can counsel." (I knew pastors and ministers did a lot of counseling, and I'd never even taken a psych course.) "Finally," I intoned, sure God could not answer any of my requests but needing a clincher, "You'll have to show me that my being in the ministry will bring the greatest joy and fulfillment in my life."

That finished, I waited, but God seemed to have faded into the woodwork. I felt better thinking God would not pursue the matter.

About a week later I sat in the foyer of the motel restaurant where I worked as a short order chef. I was studying my Bible. People passed in and out of the restaurant, and suddenly a man walked over to me and said, "Are you a Jesus freak?" ("Jesus freak" was a common term then, used to describe new Christians who had come out of the hippie movement.)

I cleared my throat and said, "Yes, sort of, but I just like to call myself a Christian."

He said, "You know, I've heard about that. Would you tell me about it?"

This struck me as unusual, but I began laying out the details of how I became a Christian—something I'd told friends about many times. Other members of his party showed up and he called them over. "Hey, listen to this guy. This is really interesting." Now six people surrounded me, and to make myself heard, I stood and continued my testimony session. You know what happens in a restaurant foyer. People saunter in and out, and several of those groups joined my little conclave. Soon about twenty people gathered around me listening. I had not vomited, and in fact I was enjoying it!

After I finished, the man thanked me and said I was a pretty good speaker, and everyone left. I didn't give an altar call or anything, but as I sat down, I remembered my prayer of a week before. I said, "Lord, you didn't do that, did you?" I shook my head. "No way!" I said, sure this was just a fluke. Next time a group got around me, I'd probably throw up right on the spot! Still, I was intrigued. I enjoyed the feeling of having twenty people listening to my testimony.

The next event occurred in the kitchen as a coworker, Kris, and I made lunch. Kris hated me. She lived with a guy named Joel, who I'd talked with a lot about being a Christian and why I believed premarital sex was wrong. She'd once threatened me with a knife, saying that if I didn't "lay off her boyfriend," she would "sneak into my room some night and cut me open like a Christmas turkey!" That didn't stop me, though I did avoid direct confrontations with her.

This particular day was a bad one for Kris. Her ex-boyfriend had shown up—the guy who used to beat her—and the motel owner had hired him as the handyman. Terror marked Kris's face, and I sympathized. We talked about fear, and I told her how becoming a Christian had rid me of many of the fears I'd had as a nonbeliever—fears like never getting married, being ugly, dying and going to hell. While we made sandwiches, I explained the gospel. At the end I said, "Would you like to ask Jesus to come into your life?"

She answered, "I just did—while you were talking. And he's there! I can feel him!"

I was stunned. Immediately that little voice reminded me, "By the way, that was the second part of your prayer, remember?"

Yeah, I remembered. But there were still two other points in that prayer, and certainly God couldn't create a counseling session out of midair! But even if he did, I was sure he couldn't convince me that the ministry could be a joy and adventure.

The next event on God's calendar happened in the foyer again. While

I sat on a couch reading *Satan Is Alive and Well on Planet Earth,* by Hal Lindsey, a woman stepped in from skiing and slumped down on the couch opposite me. She could see the cover of my book—I always held up the covers of my Christian books as I read, hoping it would start a conversation for Christ. Suddenly she sniffled and began crying. I put down the book and looked at her. "Are you all right, ma'am?"

She said, "I noticed the book you're reading and I wonder if you're a Christian."

"Yes, I am."

"I have such a problem in my life," she continued. She explained that her son had gotten involved in the occult, developed schizophrenic symptoms and ended up in a dead-end job with a life going nowhere. All of his potential had been sucked out, and now he lived as a waste of a human being, with no future and a dismal past.

I felt pained for her. I wanted to help, but I knew nothing about demon exorcism or anything like that. Moreover, her son was far away at home, so I couldn't help him.

She gazed at me with teary eyes, saying, "I just don't know what to do anymore. We came up here to have some fun and get away from it all, but I feel as bad as I ever did. Do you think you can help me?"

I didn't have a clue what to say or where to start, but I walked over to her couch and sat down next to her, praying for God to show me some verse or truth I could give to her. I opened my Bible, flipping pages and looking for something, anything. I had recently memorized Proverbs 3:5-6 and latched on to it.

> *Trust in the LORD with all your heart*
> *and lean not on your own understanding;*
> *in all your ways acknowledge him,*
> *and he will make your paths straight.*

I turned to that text, read it to her and told her what I believed it meant and how it could help her through her problem.

She asked probing questions. Answers came to me as if I had received a sudden infusion with "brains of heaven." Other texts came to mind; I showed her those and we talked about her son. It turned into a marvelous time of fellowship. When she had to go, we prayed. And then she dropped the bomb. She said, "You know, you're really good. You should be a counselor."

As she left smiling, I sat there stunned. God had done it. The first three prayers had been answered. I could speak in public. I could lead people to Christ. And I could counsel. What was worse, I felt energized by it all. I was happy. *Joyful. Fulfilled.*

The reality filled me and I was too amazed to speak. But finally I said, "Okay, God, you win. I'll go to seminary." Tears filled my eyes and relief flooded my soul. The greatest question of my life as a new Christian had been answered. And I had been a believer for only five months.

Compared to Hannah's prayer, this event ranks somewhere between the almost spiritual and the semispiritual. But it was real to me at the time. I had reached the point of relinquishing my dream of being a poet and professor in response to God's obvious desire for me to go into the ministry.

Suddenly I had a goal, something to work toward and live for. For the first time I saw that God truly was leading me into the abundant life he'd promised. I realized he was in charge of my life and had a plan for it, the plan I'd heard about many times but wasn't really sure applied to me. I felt deeply grateful that he had spoken to me that day a month earlier. I bowed my head with tears in my eyes, saying over and over, "Thank you. Thank you."

Over the next few years, God began to work in my life to make me grow spiritually. I went to seminary, faced some hard times, went through some difficult ministerial situations. But today I see that he was leading every step of the way—the same way he led Hannah to her moment of submission and hope.

THE GOD WHO GIVES

I have found that in many ways God has a plain plan for each of us: he simply wants to bless us with the things in life that will make our lives beautiful, memorable and well worth living. Like a loving father, he wants to shower us with gifts because that is his nature. He is a gift giver.

But sometimes he has to withhold an immediate blessing in order to give us a greater blessing. I believe God withheld success in the pastorate from me because he was leading me to become a writer, teacher and speaker. He withheld children from Hannah because he wanted to give her the greater blessing of a Samuel. After him, she perhaps would have other sons and daughters. But the first was a Samuel.

Do you wish for something from God? Do you have something deep within you—a dream, hope, something you've thought about for years—that you know only God could grant? Do you long for a blessing that repeatedly eludes you but that you believe only God could give, if he chose?

The guidelines are simple. Ask and keep asking. Seek and keep seeking. Knock and keep knocking. When no answer comes, wait, grow, let God build you in character and then ask again. Keep asking until he either shows you it's time to stop, he gives an unequivocal no or he answers with a resounding yes. Refuse to give up. Let him know why he should grant this gift. Repeat to him the words of the Bible, if necessary, to convince him of your determination. Refuse to let him go until he blesses you, as Jacob did when wrestling with the angel.

What if even then he does not grant you this blessing? Then maybe you need to consider doing what Hannah did. Demonstrate to God that you are willing to give up what you treasure most to fulfill his will. Then wait. Give God time to work. And walk daily in the expectation that this could be the day when your life changes forever for the good.

That's what Hannah did. God answered. And her life was transformed forever. Do that, and your relinquishment will not seem much like a relinquishment at all. It will seem more like the greatest blessing you've ever received.

GETTING HONEST

1. Think of something you've asked God for over and over with no satisfaction. Do you feel God has said no to this request? If not, if you still think he could say yes, refuse to give up on it. Storm heaven and get friends praying with you for this thing.

2. What do you need to relinquish to God's control?

3. Do you see God working in your life? Is it possible that he has withheld this blessing you want because he wants to give you a greater blessing? Ask him to bless you in the way he wishes to and look forward to seeing that blessing come—perhaps soon.

4

THE PRAYER OUT OF DOUBT
God Will Give You What You Need

A week later [Jesus'] disciples were in the house again, and Thomas was with them. Though the doors were locked, Jesus came and stood among them and said, "Peace be with you!" Then he said to Thomas, "Put your finger here; see my hands. Reach out your hand and put it into my side. Stop doubting and believe."

Thomas said to him, "My Lord and my God!"

Then Jesus told him, "Because you have seen me, you have believed; blessed are those who have not seen and yet have believed."

JOHN 20:26-29

I BEGAN STUDIES AT Dallas Theological Seminary in September 1973. For the first two years I cruised on a psychological high of excellent teaching, joyous ministry and an effervescent faith. I loved everything I was learning. Much of my faith at that stage was built on my feelings. God felt near. I talked with him all the time in my heart and otherwise. He led me through difficult situations, classes and family differences onto a new plane of life that seemed fulfilling, enlarging and enthralling.

During my third year in seminary, a crushing depression squeezed the faith out of me and replaced it with a gnawing sense of abandonment. God suddenly seemed distant, and all the good feelings flew out the door. The spiritual fellowship I'd thrived on for three years had vanished. Where was God? What had happened? What was wrong? Those questions sailed through my mind, firing depth charges of doubt into the deepest waters of my faith.

If God was no longer real to me, I wondered, why was I a Christian? Other excruciating questions surfaced as well: How could I be sure Jesus was really God? What about the Bible and all those problem passages (which I had been learning about in seminary)? How could I really trust that it was the Word of God? What convinced me that Jesus had risen from the dead? As I read the narratives, they all seemed so contradictory. And the biggie: Did God truly exist? After all, maybe my earlier "faith" had just been a roller-coaster ride of emotion, not the real thing.

I fired these questions at my friends and at my stalwart roommate, Cliff Rapp, who tried to help me think through what I was really asking and saying. But the depression lingered, the issues festered and I considered leaving school. How could I be a pastor if I wasn't even sure God existed?

Cliff suggested that I read some of the great apologetic texts by Josh McDowell, Norman Geisler, John Warwick Montgomery, Cornelius Van Til and others, and get myself "regrounded" in my beliefs. He said I needed to base my faith on facts and not feelings.

I worked at it. I read every book I could find that tackled the questions that ransacked my soul. Often I found powerful arguments that solidified my convictions that God really existed, the Bible could be trusted and Jesus was the same yesterday and today and forever.

But I still felt empty, depressed and spiritually razed. Though I found many of the answers to be virtually unarguable, God remained distant. My faith became embedded in rock and inscribed on my heart with solid, secure facts. But I felt dry, dull and hurting. No amount of data seemed to satisfy my longing for communion with the living God.

Years later I would write a book about this experience, called *The Storm Within*. Interviewing various profs and teachers, as well as men and women who had weathered their own "dark nights of the soul," I learned about a principle of the Christian life called "consolation and desolation." The theory goes like this: God works in us through two major processes, namely, consolation (that is, comfort, nearness, joy and peace) and desolation (that is, the withdrawal of conscious presence, a feeling of abandonment and the idea that God has exited from our lives).

I found this illustrated in *The Screwtape Letters* by C. S. Lewis and also his profound duel with grief in *A Grief Observed*. In both, Lewis referred to the experience of the "troughs" in which the Christian feels as if God has deserted him or her, emotions slide into depression and life becomes difficult. Lewis believed that these troughs bring the greatest growth in the believer's life. Why? Because in the troughs the believer learns what it means to obey even when he or she doesn't want to, to believe even when all feelings scream otherwise and to persevere even though every moment he or she wants to quit.

It made sense to me. I came to see myself as going through a period of desolation or being in the troughs, for I was persevering even though everything in my soul shrieked that God had deserted me and I should give it up. Perhaps you've also endured this. Thomas, the "doubter" in Scripture, did.

THE GREAT DOUBTER

Amazingly, while we call Thomas "Doubting Thomas," really all the disciples were doubters. None of them believed Jesus had risen from the dead until they actually saw him alive and well. But Thomas hadn't been present at the first appearances, and that put him in the position of the lone "doubter" for a short while.

Consider the few things we know about Thomas. The most important data come from two experiences that reveal Thomas's outlook and character. The first, in John 11, depicts Jesus' conversation with his disciples about Lazarus's illness. At that time it was very dangerous for Jesus to travel in Judea because of the hostility of the Pharisees and Sadducees. When he heard of Lazarus's illness, though, Jesus waited several days before traveling to Bethany to see Lazarus in person.

This exchange takes place with Jesus and his disciples in John 11:

[Jesus] said to his disciples, "Let us go back to Judea."

"But Rabbi," they said, "a short while ago the Jews tried to stone you, and yet you are going back there?"

Jesus answered, "Are there not twelve hours of daylight? A man who walks by day will not stumble, for he sees by this world's light. It is when he walks by night that he stumbles, for he has no light."

After he had said this, he went on to tell them, "Our friend Lazarus has fallen asleep; but I am going there to wake him up."

His disciples replied, "Lord, if he sleeps, he will get better." Jesus had been speaking of his death, but his disciples thought he meant natural sleep.

So then he told them plainly, "Lazarus is dead, and for your sake I am glad I was not there, so that you may believe. But let us go to him." (verses 7-15)

The conversation shows that Jesus planned to go to Lazarus at that point, even though he had died and even though the Jews still wanted to stone Jesus. Then Thomas makes an amazing comment: "Thomas (called Didymus) said to the rest of the disciples, 'Let us also go, that we may die with him' " (verse 16).

Clearly Thomas would rather die with Jesus than stay behind without him. What exactly do Thomas's words reveal here? Jesus had become his whole life and world. He preferred death to the thought of not being with Jesus. Thomas craved that fellowship, friendship and worship more than anything else in his life.

Thomas had counted the cost. He knew what it meant to follow Jesus. His old life was gone and he had no desire to return to it as Peter and the fishermen did after the resurrection. I don't mean Thomas was more committed than the others, only that he understood Jesus' mission. He saw that Jesus would probably die for this cause he had championed. Thomas simply didn't understand the real finale, with Jesus rising from the dead.

Many Christians discover this reality when they trust Christ: he has become everything to them. To die is better than to live without him.

Gloria Swanson, famed actress in Hollywood's early days, became a Christian in her later years. She once said on a Merv Griffin show, "I had everything, but I never had peace of mind until I found God." She had experienced something of what Thomas had—the things of this world became meaningless next to the glory of knowing God.

I love the back cover text from J. I. Packer's *Knowing God*:

> *What were we made for?*
>> *To know God.*
> *What aim should we set ourselves in life?*
>> *To know God.*
> *What is the eternal life that Jesus gives?*
>> *Knowledge of God.*
> *What is the best thing in life?*
>> *Knowledge of God.*
> *What in a man gives God most pleasure?*
>> *Knowledge of Himself.*

Thomas could have written that. Jesus stood for everything Thomas wanted in life, and being close to him was all that mattered.

SHOW ME THE WAY

We also read about Thomas in John 14 when Jesus tells the disciples that if they have seen him, they have also seen the Father. Here, Jesus says:

Do not let your hearts be troubled. Trust in God; trust also in me. In my Father's house are many rooms; if it were not so, I would have told you. I am going there to prepare a place for you. And if I go and prepare a place for you, I will come back and take you to be with me that you also may be where I am. You know the way to the place where I am going. (John 14:1-4)

Obviously this is a revealing statement, but Thomas's lone comment is even more revealing. He says, "Lord, we don't know where you are going, so how can we know the way?" (verse 5). What do we see here?

Again, scholars speak of Thomas's obsession with being close to Jesus. If Jesus was going somewhere, Thomas wanted to go there too. Thomas lived for only one thing: to be near Jesus, listen to his words and see him healing, helping and transforming people.

As a result, when we come to Thomas's display of doubt after the resurrection, we can understand why he wasn't with the other disciples. Jesus' death shattered Thomas's world. He had put his everything on the line with Jesus, and now all was gone. He was devastated. What could he do now? He knew he couldn't go back to his old life. So he went out alone to think and brood and perhaps to pray. Maybe he didn't want to be bothered by the others, because his grief was too great and he didn't want them to see it. He appears to have been a loner to begin with, and maybe this was the only way he could deal with his pain.

When the disciples saw Jesus raised and met with him in the upper room, naturally they had to tell Thomas. But how did Thomas react? He told them, "Unless I see the nail marks in his hands and put my finger where the nails were, and put my hand into his side, I will not believe it" (John 20:25). Why this reaction? Wasn't this the hope Thomas had wanted? I think it was a classic reaction of "I'm too depressed. Don't try and cheer me up with a story."

Thomas was a stickler for the facts. When Jesus planned to travel to Lazarus's tomb, Thomas was ready to go and die. The cost was plain to him. When Jesus told them he would soon leave them and go to his Father's house, Thomas wanted to know the way. Details. Reality. Thomas could bear no fictions.

That's why he said what he did. Although he could see the disciples' joy and confidence, for him it had to be a sure thing. No mistakes. No pretenses. No fakery. "Give me the real thing. Let me see Jesus with his scars and all. Let me touch him, and then I'll be sure. This grief hurts so much that I can't suddenly entertain hope and then have it all dashed to pieces again."

I think I know how Thomas must have felt.

When I was fourteen years old, my grandfather died. Grandpop Littleton meant more to me than any of my other relatives. He taught me to bait a hook, catch a fish, scale it and cook it. He gave me my first jackknife.

The year Grandpop retired, he and Grandmom took a trip from New Jersey out west with car and trailer. I went with them. There we bought firecrackers—the number-one love of every twelve-year-old boy—and Grandpop and I set them off at our campsites. I blew up many anthills in those days.

That same year, when the end of summer came and it was time to stock firewood for the winter months, Grandpop, my father and I sawed up the dead trees in the area and trundled them home in Grandpop's truck. Grandpop showed me how to wield an ax, sledgehammer and wedge to split the logs into burnable chunks. I remember many times when Grandpop set the wedge on top of a mammoth log and I stood with the sledgehammer, worried I'd hit his hand. He'd shout, "Sock it! Go ahead and sock it!"

I'd wail, "I'm afraid to hit your hand."

"My hand won't be there," he'd chide me. "What—you think I'm some kind of dumb bunny? When you swing, at the last second I pull my hand away, but the wedge still stands. So go ahead, sock it." Grandpop taught me much of the confidence I have today as a Christian.

The night he died of a stroke, I cried myself to sleep. But the funeral was worse. All those people saying wonderful things about him, and him lying in that casket, looking very dead, destroyed me. I kept running into the bathroom to cry because I didn't want people to see a fourteen-year-old boy bawling his eyes out.

After the pastor spoke at the funeral, he asked the whole family to walk past the casket to say goodbye to Grandpop. That became the worst experience of my life. Somehow at that moment it all became real in a way it hadn't before. "Saying goodbye" stuck in my mind, and I realized I'd never see him again. I wasn't a Christian then (though he was), and even though people told me he was in heaven, I had no such belief or conviction myself.

I lost it. Passing the casket, fighting the feeling of my face twisting with grief, I finally burst into tears. I felt as lonely and lost as I've ever felt in my life. When my grandfather died, he took everything. I felt as if my life didn't matter anymore.

Sometimes I wonder if that was like the reaction Thomas had to Jesus' death. Yet this was worse because Thomas was an adult and he understood the ramifications of what had happened. If people had visited me, saying they had seen my Grandpop alive, something inside me might have sprung up in hope. But perhaps something else would have denied it. "Don't make me hope this! I've been through too much to be dashed down again."

I believe that was at least part of why Thomas reacted as he did to the disciples' story.

JESUS' REACTION

Here we find one of the most wondrous moments in Scripture. Thomas was waiting with the disciples in the upper room and sud-

denly Jesus materialized. What did Jesus do? Scold Thomas because
he didn't believe the disciples? Preach a sermon against doubt? Joke
with Thomas a little, saying, "Hey, what's the problem here?" No,
Jesus walked to Thomas immediately and said, "Put your finger here;
see my hands. Reach out your hand and put it into my side. Stop
doubting and believe" (John 20:27).

Jesus didn't condemn Thomas for having doubts. Nor did he chide
the disciple for wanting to see his wounds, as if Jesus might fake his
own death. No, Jesus gave Thomas permission to explore the facts
until his doubts were quelled.

I know Christians who worry that if they have a doubt, Jesus will
sling them out of the kingdom. In many cases they have read the passage in James 1 about doubt: "When [a man] asks [God for some-
thing], he must believe and not doubt, because he who doubts is like
a wave of the sea, blown and tossed by the wind. That man should
not think he will receive anything from the Lord; he is a double-
minded man, unstable in all he does" (James 1:6-8). And because of
these verses, they believe that doubt is an ultimate sin, akin to the
blasphemy of the Holy Spirit. I know others, who, because of their
doubts, are kept from a full, committed faith and meander in life,
never experiencing God's true power in their hearts. But Jesus blew
all those thoughts to pieces with Thomas.

And what was Thomas's reaction? He fell at Jesus' feet, crying, "My
Lord and my God!" (John 20:28). This is one of the most definitive
statements of belief in Jesus' deity that we find in the New Testament.
Jesus' proof turned Thomas completely around and satisfied the
deepest longings of his soul. He was restored to full faith and would
never again slide into abject grief because he felt all was lost.

Thomas is a good guide for us in terms of getting honest with God
about our doubts. If you're having doubt, here are some principles to

remember: (1) Voice your concern; ask God the questions you need answered. (2) Expect God to answer in a straightforward, convincing way. (3) Anticipate that God's answers will make you fall in renewed worship at his feet.

WILD HOPE

I don't think doubt is an uncommon problem. All of us wrestle with doubts at times, and to ignore them invites peril.

In *Disappointment with God* author Philip Yancey tells the story of Richard, who had experienced much devastation in his life: the breakup of a love relationship, loss of relatives through death, financial reversals and so on. Richard initially asked Yancey to endorse a book about Job he was working on. Yancey read it, enjoyed it and thought it was brilliant. He endorsed it heartily. Sometime later, when the book was ready to be published, Richard called Philip and told him he didn't believe in the God he'd written about in h's book anymore and he wanted to tell Philip why.

In response to what he heard from Richard, Yancey raises three powerful issues that all of us wrestle with sooner or later: Is God unfair? Is he silent? Is he hidden? Yancey also comes to some conclusions: Yes, sometimes it appears that God is unfair. Yes, sometimes he is silent. Yes, sometimes he is hidden. We will all struggle through times when these are the circumstances of our faith and life.

The book ends with two stories. One is the story of a son who murders his father because he hates him so much. Later, though, in the detention unit, a guard passes the boy's room and hears him sob, "I want my father. I want my father." It's a stunning portrait. Boy kills father, then wants him back because he misses and loves the man so.

Yancey concludes that, like that boy, the modern world has in many ways rejected God because he sometimes seems unfair, is occasionally silent and is frequently hidden. People "murder" God in their hearts. At the same time, they wish they could know and see God, to make it right, to make the murder never happen. But they can't. They live on in the horror of what they have become—guilty people who can't seem to move toward God while longing for the truth he will bring into their lives. Yancey posits that such people have hard lives, saying, "The alternative to disappointment with God seems to be disappointment without God."

Thomas, like Philip Yancey's friend, could have ended up like that. So could I as I trudged through my clinical depression. I felt God was unfair to let me go through doubt and depression. I considered him hideously withdrawn and silent, letting me plod my way through darkness with no idea of where I was going. And he seemed coldly hidden to all my pleas.

For Thomas, what happened to Jesus on the cross was incredibly unfair. How could God allow such a thing? On the dark days between the cross and Jesus' revelation to Thomas, there was silence. Jesus was dead. Where was God, the one who was supposedly the Father of Jesus? And he was hidden—gone, disappeared, dead. It must have been an agonizing time for Thomas, sitting alone in his darkness with nothing ahead of him but life without Christ. Despair, depression, relentless pain and rank hopelessness were all Thomas thought he had to look forward to.

He and I could have ended up horribly disfigured as believers, sadly going through the motions of religion but missing the true gutsy, sure and sustaining hope of resurrection, heaven, eternal life and fellowship with Jesus forever. But we didn't continue in that condition, because God did something. For Thomas, Jesus appeared with unequivocal proof that he was the resurrected Lord of the universe. For me, my questions were soon given fact-fired answers that stoked my faith back to normal. I eventually came out of my darkness and depression, and as a result of my doubts, my faith was grounded, fixed in the very earth of Scripture and truth, not just a vague feeling of God's presence and love.

At the end of *Disappointment with God* Philip Yancey tells of how, on a visit to his mother, he discovered a crumpled photo of himself as a baby in his mother's photo collection. He asked his mother why she'd kept that creased and rumpled photo. She explained that when Philip was a baby, his father had contracted polio and was eventually forced to live in a tight body-long iron lung that helped him breathe. To give his father a morsel of joy in his endless days of fighting for each breath, she taped the photo of Philip in a tiny slot on the machine above her husband's head so he could see Philip all the time. She did the same with photos of herself and Philip's brother.

Yancey wonders what his father did in those hours when he struggled for breath and could only gaze on his family's pictures. Did he pray? Did he love his family? Yancey concludes that his father undoubtedly did pray and love his family, but that was just about all he could do. He died during Yancey's early childhood. Yancey speculates that perhaps his father is doing the same things now in heaven.

Throughout the book Yancey speaks of his own doubts and struggles with disappointment as a student in college. He finally came to faith and later realized his experience was a stunning example of what he was writing about in his book. He had a man in his past whom the grown Philip Yancey had never known personally and who, like God, was silent and hidden but was still there, loving, caring, remembering. Yancey concludes, "The emotions I felt when my mother showed me the crumpled photo were the very same emotions I felt that February night in a college dorm room when I first believed in a God of love. *Someone is there,* I realized. *Someone is watching life*

as it unfolds on this planet. More, Someone is there who loves me. . . . It
was a startling feeling of wild hope, a feeling so new and overwhelming that it seemed fully worth risking my life on."

What do you do when you face doubts? Tell God about them. Lay
them out before him. Press him for answers to the parts of it that can
receive answers. Trust him to come through, to answer you in such a
way that you will have full assurance. And keep laying those doubts
at his feet when they arise. He loves you too much to leave you
stranded on the end of a doubt. Rather, when you cry out to him, he
will pull you out of its darkness and into his perfect, beautiful, en-
folding light.

A Question Out of the Dark

One day in my own darkness, I asked my roommate, Cliff, "Where is
God? Why doesn't he answer me? Why has he left me like this?"

Cliff responded, "I don't know what to tell you, Mark, except the
truth: God is real. I know. And I know he loves you and he loves me.
I don't know exactly how I know these things, except from the Bible
and from my own experience. But I guarantee you that there is some
reason for what you're feeling. And one day God will lift your darkness and you'll feel fine again. But there will be one great difference:
you will be stronger in faith, stronger in your convictions and a stronger person for God's kingdom because of it. That I am sure of. That's
what I'm praying for."

Perhaps at that moment my friend Cliff was given the gift of
prophecy. I don't know. But I do know it all came true. I know God
did make me a far stronger Christian as a result of my doubts. I also
know that God is good, that he doesn't shrink from our harsh questions and that he wants us to know he still loves us infinitely even
when we doubt him. Nothing can take that love away from us—not

our doubts, not our darkness, nothing—not even ourselves.

Get honest with God about your doubts. Don't hide them. Fire them at him until he answers, because he promises to answer in a way that you will know is his work. That is, for me—and I hope for you—stout comfort.

GETTING HONEST

1. What doubts do you face? Get them onto paper in question form and then pray over them, asking God to answer speedily and with the brilliance only he can bring to questions like that.

2. What do you do with doubts that persist? Getting honest with God means walking in relationship. Because he doesn't answer today doesn't mean he won't answer ever. Persist in your fellowship with him and keep laying those doubts at his feet. As with Thomas, he does not condemn but wants only to bless you with the truth that sets a heart free.

5

THE PRAYER OF DEEP DISAPPOINTMENT
Remember, You Aren't Home Yet

The LORD said, "Go out and stand on the mountain in the presence of the LORD, for the LORD is about to pass by."

Then a great and powerful wind tore the mountains apart and shattered the rocks before the LORD but the LORD was not in the wind. After the wind there was an earthquake, but the LORD was not in the earthquake. After the earthquake came a fire, but the LORD was not in the fire. And after the fire came a gentle whisper. When Elijah heard it, he pulled his cloak over his face and went out and stood at the mouth of the cave.

Then a voice said to him, "What are you doing here, Elijah?"

1 KINGS 19:11-13

HAVE YOU EVER WANTED TO see God do something big? Something that gets the notice of the community, maybe even the world? Something that would have everyone talking—lives changed, families reunited, messed-up people turned around for good?

As an aspiring pastor, I dreamed of having an effective ministry that would connect people with Christ. Ever since I'd become a Christian, one thing had become paramount in my mind: the joy and exhilaration of knowing Jesus personally. In every ministry I've ever been part of, that was my vision—to show people how to experience the fullness of God's love, power, joy and presence. Not that I was some kind of master at it. It's just that when I met Christ for the first time, so many things changed in my life. I knew what the world was all about for the first time. I knew how I fit into it. And I knew God was going to take me out of it to another one far more magnificent when I died.

As a result, every day I arose with a sense of expectation and excitement that God would use me in his great adventure. I burned to help every lonely, forgotten, hurting, lost person to know that he or she didn't have to remain that way. In my mind the best way to do that was to be a pastor. Working in the trenches. Meeting people where they lived. Becoming part of the lives of those who were as broken and scared as I was before I met Christ. However, I left the pastorate in 1984 for various reasons, including marital challenges.

Over the years I tried to get back into it, but my divorce in 1993 seemed to seal my fate. I felt no one would ever again consider me for a ministerial position. Not being a pastor, though, nagged at my soul. Was I supposed to be one or not?

After I remarried in 1996, my wife, Jeanette, told me, "If you want to go back into the ministry, I'll be with you in it." So in 1998 I embarked on what I thought would be the great ministry of my life. My wife and I were directors of Christian education in a church when a contemporary-style church asked me to be their pastor. The congregation was small, but it seemed like a manageable size for me.

At the start it was immensely gratifying. Within six months, though, things went sour. We learned that the church had split several times before we'd arrived there. And now some people had become critical and others left the church, telling us they just couldn't go through more trouble. Eventually the few people left decided to merge with another, slightly larger church. The larger church offered me an associate pastor position, but I honestly didn't feel led to do that. Around that same time, without even seeking it, my wife was offered a great job with *Moody Magazine* in Chicago. We decided to move to Chicago, where I would continue writing and speaking.

As we settled in our new home, I wondered if God would ever make a ministry work under my leadership. My writing ministry was doing fine, but I still longed for a solid pastorate. I decided I'd explore a part-time position in a smaller church. I found just such a church in the Chicago area. They had a nice building, a solid core of about thirty members and a black-ink budget, and they wanted someone part time who could build a ministry. With a good location in the community, the church also had a fine praise band, and the people seemed supportive and eager. It looked like a perfect position for what I longed to do.

They offered me the job. After much prayer and consideration, I accepted it. Before my first day of work, though, I prayed a prayer that was somewhat strange for me but that I sincerely felt deep in my heart. I said, "Lord, if you want me in the pastorate, I believe this is the one. I've had some discouraging ministry experiences. This is my last shot. If you don't want me in this, make it end fast before I really get hooked into the people. Then I'll know that you want me in writing and other work, not the pastorate." I didn't think much about that prayer at first. But later I would realize that God had taken me most seriously.

My first month in the church, December, was uneventful as a few visitors came and I started developing relationships with various members. On Christmas Eve I preached what I felt was a creative, interesting sermon, using lighted candles to accent the message. Afterward people seemed excited and happy, and I went home bolstered by a wave of expectation. I sensed that we were on the cusp of something amazing. I believed the miracle ministry of helping people connect with God would soon happen.

The first week of January, though, it all came apart. Certain members of the church expressed disaffection with my ministry. They felt my mentioning sin and salvation, especially around the holidays, would turn off the seekers they hoped to reach. I was astonished at this reaction, as were some others in the church. The next weeks brought several intense meetings with the board. I ended up resigning after being there only two months.

When I got home on the afternoon I resigned, I felt devastated. God had answered my prayer in ways I didn't expect or want, but it finalized my own commitment in my mind. I would not seek a pastorate again. My primary ministry and career would be in writing and speaking, the areas in which God was opening doors. But ever since my call to the ministry over twenty-eight years before, I had believed God wanted me to pastor. This was the crowning blow. My dream was extinguished, and in my heart I felt lost.

THE END OF THE DREAM

Have you ever dreamed a dream, however big or small, and had it all come to nothing?

I know a Christian man who wanted to start an Italian restaurant that would minister to people as well as feed them. They served great food. But the founder's belief in helping people meant he would not serve liquor. The restaurant lasted less than two years before he went bankrupt.

I have met many lovely folks who have dreamed for years of getting married and having children. One woman is a close friend. When she and my wife get together, it always comes around to her pain in not finding a mate. This woman has a great career, she's beautiful, she is deeply involved in ministry, and she would by all rights be a prime catch for any man. Yet she is unmarried, and at forty her time for having children is running out.

Speaking at writers conferences, I meet many hopeful writers with grand dreams. They're sure their book will set God's kingdom afire. Yet many face only rejection and more rejection each year. Or they have some success in getting a book or books published, but none of them sell many copies, and they're soon dropped by their once-enthusiastic publishers.

I know Christians who have loved and followed God for all their lives. They've contributed to his work immeasurably. They've made sacrifices. But the one dream they've always had—that ministry that grows like wildfire or that music career that brightens everyone's day—has never come true. In some cases they simply shrug it off.

Others struggle. This dream has been with them for decades. It's fueled every sacrifice they've made. It's rooted in them as deeply as a sequoia. And yet as the years wing by, the chances of its ever happening become more and more slight.

Where do such discouraged believers go? Do they slip into a midlife crisis about it? Do they recede into bitterness, feeling God has reneged on every promise he ever made in Scripture? Do they run to the local bar and get drunk?

Is it ever good to dream and pray and hope for something in life, simple or great, and have it never come to be?

In the context of such thoughts I always turn to Elijah, a prophet who learned in a hard way what getting honest with God is all about. In him we discover one of the great conversations with God about God's way of working in the world. In him we see the big bubble bursting and the man, crippled with disappointment, receding into the woodwork. But in his story we also learn a great truth that can repower anyone who has seen his or her bubble burst.

ELIJAH'S SHOWDOWN

We meet Elijah first in 1 Kings 17, where we read that he was so incensed with King Ahab's conduct that he prayed for a famine on the land. Elijah interceded with such power, in fact, that God didn't send a rain in over three years. Various miracles followed, including Elijah's being fed by ravens, God's miraculously providing more food through a poor widow and Elijah's raising the widow's son from the dead.

Elijah was a prophet familiar with God's power and miracles. He and his protégé, Elisha, were the first and only miracle workers in the Old Testament since the days of Moses. Only Jesus and the apostles would outdo this duo for majestic works in the life of Israel.

When God finally told Elijah to visit King Ahab and tell him that God had relented and would send rain on the earth, Elijah obeyed. But as he went through the motions, something happened in the heart of Elijah. He began to see the possibility of an incredible revival, the thing he'd dreamed about for years.

Elijah cooked up a grand plan in which he would confront the idolaters in Israel—the 450 prophets of Baal and the 400 prophets of Asherah, the two chief false deities worshiped in the land at that time. Elijah gathered them on Mount Carmel, where he proposed a little test to see what Baal could do and what the living God could do. Only the true God could answer in such a test.

You probably know the story. In the confrontation between Elijah and the errant prophets, two sacrifices were set up—one for Baal, the god of weather, thunder and lightning, and one for Jehovah, the omnipotent true God of the Hebrews. Elijah offered the false prophets the first stab at this impressive and original stage play.

The prophets set up their altar and cried out to Baal to send a bolt of lightning and ignite the bull lying on the stones and wood. After all, lightning was what Baal specialized in, wasn't it? The prophets danced, pled with Baal, cut themselves with knives, tore their robes. Baal did nothing. Meanwhile, Elijah taunted them. "Shout louder! . . . Perhaps he is deep in thought, or busy, or traveling. Maybe he is sleeping and must be awakened" (1 Kings 18:27). For a full day these illegitimate prophets danced, shouted and spilled their blood. All to no avail.

Finally it was Elijah's turn. The crowd became hushed, their eyes fixed on the prophet. In a dramatic display Elijah laid out the altar with twelve stones, symbolizing the tribes of Israel. He dug a trench around the altar, placed wood on top of the stones and finally added the pieces of a bull that were supposed to be incinerated. At the end, with a flourish, he had some men run by the local stream, fill four large pitchers with water and pour it over the bull. This he did three times, until the bull was drenched and the trench had become a moat.

With every eye on him, Elijah lifted his hands to heaven and prayed a simple prayer, asking God to ignite the sacrifice. He had no more than finished the last syllable when a lightning bolt blasted out of the blue and burned up the bull, wood, altar and water in one magnificent explosion of light and power. There was nothing but a large smudge left as the people fell on their knees and cried out, "The LORD—he is God! The LORD—he is God!" Elijah immediately took charge and commanded the men to grab all the ridiculous idolatrous prophets—850 of them—and then Elijah dragged them down to the stream, where he had their heads hacked off.

Don't you wish you had been there? This was surely the launching point of the greatest revival in Israel's history, wasn't it? Isn't that what Elijah had dreamed of? Isn't this what he'd wanted to see since he'd originally become the miracle-working prophet of Jehovah?

You would think so, wouldn't you?

ELIJAH'S LETDOWN

After the great prophetic duel, Elijah told Ahab to get moving because the biggest rainstorm in Israel's history would soon inundate the land. Elijah climbed to the top of Mount Carmel, prayed in the storm and then raced down the road, outrunning Ahab in his chariot on the way to his palace in Jezreel.

Elijah may have expected that Ahab would order the main cause of all Israel's idolatry, Queen Jezebel, out of his house. Surely Ahab would then rush out to Elijah, make him his number-one prophet and adviser, and then ask what he should do now that he was an ardent believer in Jehovah. But it didn't happen. Instead Jezebel issued a summons for Elijah's arrest and swore that she would part his head from his shoulders just as he'd done with her prophets.

What do you think Elijah's reaction to this turn of affairs would be? Elijah had just caused and been witness to one of the great miracles of history. He had personally exterminated 850 idol-worshiping prophets. He had footraced from Mount Carmel to Jezreel—over twenty miles—and beaten a maniac in a chariot. Would you expect this prophet to cut and run because some woman threatened him? You might expect him to shout something like "Hack her head off, too, and make it a complete wipeout." But no. For a second Elijah stood there, amazed, nonplused, befuddled, trying to reason through what was happening. "Didn't God just . . . ?" "Didn't I just . . . ?" "What is happening, Lor—?" And then he ran.

He dashed away from the palace gates, careened through the land to Beersheba, a city of Judah, over one hundred miles away. There he collapsed under a broom tree, asked God to let him die and fell asleep. After Elijah spent perhaps several hours in sleep, an angel (some believe he was Jesus Christ in angelic disguise) appeared and fed Elijah a cake baked over a fire the angel made. Elijah ate and promptly fell asleep again. The angel let him sleep, then touched him and fed him again.

This time when Elijah arose, he felt so energized by the sleep and food that he wandered for the next forty days, running and hiding, until he came to Horeb, the mountain of God (the same as Mount Sinai), about two hundred miles south of Beersheba. There he holed up in a cave, and the next morning God had the conversation with him that I see as the point of this whole escapade.

But before we get to that conversation, let's ask a question. Why did Elijah run? Was he that frightened of Jezebel? Would a man who had seen miracles, who had provoked God himself to perform one of the greatest works of power in all the Bible, have buckled so easily?

Remember several things. By that point, Elijah had become utterly exhausted. The demonstration on Mount Carmel took all day. Then the execution of possibly 850 struggling men must have taken hours. Finally, Elijah had run at least twenty miles from Mount Carmel to Jezreel. Didn't this man have a right to feel a little tired? Actually, I think Elijah was probably more energized than he'd ever been. So what happened?

I believe that Elijah expected the revival to begin the instant the miracle happened. He figured people would be hailing him all along the road. Most of all, he thought King Ahab would congratulate him and profess unending fealty to the God whom Elijah loved. None of it happened. By the time Jezebel threatened him, Elijah had probably realized the dream revival he had anticipated was not materializing. Bitter disappointment and disillusionment flooded his heart. Along with the sudden loss of adrenaline would have come a poisonous inundation of weariness and hopelessness. Ever been there?

Having gone through a divorce, I know well the emotional roller coaster people can find themselves on. At first, with the confrontation in person and possibly in court, with defending yourself, negotiating divorce agreements and so on, your senses are seized with a fury of strength, decisiveness and determination. But then it's done. You suddenly realize your whole life has been blown to bits. Perhaps, if you're the "victim" in the divorce scenario, you're smitten with a deep sense of grief and loss. The energy dissipates. All that's left is a deep-seated sense of emptiness. The dream has truly been blasted out of your mind, and in its place appears the bleak landscape of a future without hope. Everything you had you had given for that marriage. And now it's over.

It was the same for me in my failures in the pastorate. People repeatedly told me that I hadn't failed, that it was not my mistake or doing. But the fact was that what had gone up like a rocket had come down like a rock. Each time I felt devastated. The deeper feeling, though, was that God had somehow let me down. Hadn't he "called" me to these ministries, this marriage? Hadn't I sought him for days on end before embarking on these "works," asking him to grant me success? Hadn't he seemed to give me the "go ahead," encouraging me with stout crescendos of spiritual cheerleading? Hadn't I even told him that, if for some reason he didn't want me to do this, he should tell me now and spare me the agony of a later failure? God seemed to be all for it all the way. But the reality clobbered the dream on its forehead and sent it reeling into a nightmare. That can knock over anyone.

A multitude of other experiences can wreak the same sort of havoc in a Christian's life. Bankruptcy, loss of a job, discovering your mate has committed adultery, the death of a child or spouse, a criminal attack—all of these and more can cause severe disappointment in a life. God has just not turned out to be the way you thought. You started off so grandly, sails flying, and now you're lying facedown in the dirt.

Elijah had held the throttle wide open for over three years. He'd prayed down a famine, been fed by ravens and raised a kid from the dead. He'd dreamed about this revival a long time. In his heart he nurtured it, probably fantasizing about all the wondrous moments that would come out of thousands of people leaving idolatry and turning into true believers. He'd longed for it more than any other desire of his life, and now it was dead. He needed to work through all this with God.

THE GENTLE WHISPER

God did not abandon Elijah in his disappointment. He responded amid the tough and unanticipated circumstances.

The first thing to note is that God understood Elijah's pain. He did not give Elijah a lecture or a three-point lesson in revival making. He let the poor fellow sleep. Then he fed him with angelic food—food so strengthening that Elijah would roam the next forty days without need of another meal (1 Kings 19:8).

Second, God gave Elijah time to think, meditate and recuperate. That's an essential part of the process of getting honest with God. As we lay out before God our frustration, he doesn't become one of Job's counselors, berating us for our obvious failure. Nor does he shout at us, "Buck up! When the going gets tough, the tough get going." That's a wonderful slogan, and many times it works. But when disappointment smacks us flat, we don't want a sermon. We don't want a pep talk. We need rest, the time to reflect and more rest.

Finally, God gave Elijah time to wander. This wandering, as an element of getting honest in prayer, is essential. Many times in our confusion we want answers, fast and straight. But there are other times when sober reflection is called for, as well as the time to simply relax and not push ourselves. Getting honest means learning anew to speak straightforwardly to God.

God didn't ask Elijah a single question during this time (at least so far as we know). He didn't press Elijah for a report on his schedule and what he'd accomplished in the last few weeks. He held off all the sage words he must have had humming in his own mind and waited. But once Elijah nestled into the cave on Mount Horeb, a page turned and God began to perform the surgery and repair work Elijah needed to get on with the rest of his life.

God came to Elijah and gently began to talk, to get honest. It started with a question: "What are you doing here, Elijah?" (1 Kings 19:9). It's an open-ended question, a kind of divine curiosity, an invitation to talk after forty days of silence.

Elijah's disappointment and the conclusion he's come to after reliving the disaster for forty days immediately rise to the surface. Elijah knew there was no point in beating around the bush with God, so he came right out with his complaint. "I have been very zealous for the LORD God Almighty. The Israelites have rejected your covenant, broken down your altars, and put your prophets to death with the sword. I am the only one left, and now they are trying to kill me too" (1 Kings 19:10).

As we break Elijah's response down, we discover that he has actually come to three conclusions. (1) "I have been very zealous." In other words, "I served you with all my heart. I gave it my best shot, and it's come to this. So what's the point in being zealous? I thought you were on my side." (2) "The Israelites have rejected your covenant, broken down your altars, and put your prophets to death." Note the emphasis on "your." "We've been doing your work, God. For you. Not us. You. We've been preaching the truth. We've built places for the people to worship you rightly. And we've given them your word. But all they do is kill us. Just what kind of a God are you, letting your workers end in the pits?" (3) "I am the only one left, and now they are trying to kill me too." In other words, "It's your program, God. Your people, your religion. And yet you treat your most committed members like dirt. Why should any of us serve you when things go like that?"

It all comes back to what a disappointment God has proved to be to Elijah. "I thought you were almighty. I thought you could do anything. I thought you were going to use me in a grand cause. Instead, I'm running for my life." Ever been there?

"I thought you were going to come through, God, in that business venture. But obviously you didn't. Don't expect me to be tricked into doing something like this next time."

"I trusted you, Lord. I thought she was the one. Now look at what has happened! How do you expect me to trust you ever again?"

"I gave everything I had on this one, Lord. It didn't work, so I'm through. Here's my resignation letter. I'm going fishing."

We feel this way from time to time. Elijah did too. So God had to give Elijah a little object lesson about this dream he has had.

God instructed Elijah to step out of the cave and watch something. God specifically said, "Stand on the mountain in the presence of the LORD, for the LORD is about to pass by" (1 Kings 19:11). Elijah was going to get a real look at the majestic God of the universe, the first such look since Moses was hidden in the cleft of the rock and saw God's back (Exodus 33).

Elijah stood on the mountain and watched. The first thing that happened was a rushing wind so powerful the mountains were rent and the rocks split apart. However, God made it clear he wasn't in that wind. The second phenomenon was an earthquake that presumably shook the whole mountain and may have made Elijah totter. But again, God wasn't in the earthquake. The third apparition of power was an inferno of fire, probably devouring everything in its path. But once again, God wasn't in the fire.

What is the point? God was getting there. Following the fire comes a "gentle whisper" (verse 12). The same words are translated "still small voice" in the King James Version of the Bible. Elijah heard the gentle whisper so deeply in his soul that he pulled his cloak tightly about him and went to the mouth of the cave. Then God asked for the second time that day, "What are you doing here, Elijah?"

Elijah repeated what he had said the first time—"I have been very zealous for the LORD God Almighty" and so on (verse 14). Had Elijah not learned anything? Maybe he'd learned it a little too clearly. But what was it?

THE GREAT LESSON

I think Elijah's lesson is a lesson every dreamer has to learn sooner or later, and it's this: God Almighty is quite capable of doing big things, accomplishing grand and astonishing miracles in the midst of his people. He can literally do the impossible one day and then blow us away with something even more impossible the next, piling up the impossibles until all of us are out of our minds with wonder. God can do that. But that's not the primary way he works.

When God is present in a work, it's not usually like the wind, the earthquake or the inferno; it's more like a still, small voice, a gentle whisper. In other words, most of the time in life, God works subtly, quietly, without fanfare. He only rarely performs the miraculous. He very rarely knocks the world over with a stupendous event. He reserved most of that for the time of Jesus and the apostles. Since then he's simmered back down to a quiet whispering in the hearts of men and women, wooing them to himself and drawing them with the deftest, almost imperceptible actions.

Did you get that? Chances are that God will never do many of the grandiose things we dream of in our lifetimes. How many can realistically be a Billy Graham or a Mother Teresa? But millions can be just as effective in small ways in their part of the world. As Francis Schaeffer once wrote, "There are no little people." In the eyes of God, the single prayer to receive Christ in a backyard Bible club is just as significant as the thousands marching forward at an evangelistic rally. In the eyes of God, the guy who stops and helps a woman with a flat tire is just as important in his plan as Watson and Crick discovering

DNA. In the eyes of God, the little things done in little ways by little people no one has ever heard of are his great works in human history. We don't know about them now. But one day, when Christ's judgment reveals all, we will see each of our deeds in the way God sees them.

What was God saying to Elijah? "You don't have to do big things to impress me, my friend. I am quite satisfied with your daily efforts to live and walk in my will, meeting the surprises of the day with cheer and kindness and love. I am content to see you live a quiet, godly life, influencing only your little circle of friends and acquaintances. I don't require that you change the whole world in a day. For even I couldn't do it that way, or I would. Changing people's hearts is a tough business done by chipping away a little piece of hardness here and a little piece of hardness there over many years until one day the green shoot of faith pops through. It rarely happens with a front-page headline. Mostly it's not even mentioned in polite society. But it is written in my book. And that's all that matters in the end."

Should we ever dream big dreams, think in broad strokes? Sure. Why not? What harm can it do? Maybe one day your dream will be achieved and you'll write a book about it and everyone will talk about you in their front rooms. For maybe a minute. And then they'll pass on to the next big newsmaker.

Keep it in perspective. Keep it real. Don't expect God to exalt you today or tomorrow. It could happen. You humble yourself before him, love him and work hard; maybe he will exalt you in the eyes of the world one day. But wouldn't you trade that for Jesus' personal accolade and exaltation at his judgment seat before all creation? If you're realistic, you would.

I once heard a preacher tell a story about a missionary who came home from Africa on a ship that also brought Theodore Roosevelt, then president of the United States, back from one of his African safaris. As the ship docked, huge crowds of reporters clustered around the gangplanks, snapping pictures and calling out questions to the president as he disembarked. The missionary watched in amazement, then realized that there was not a single person there to greet him. Disappointed beyond words, he turned to his wife and said, "Is this what I get when I come home after years of mission work in Africa? Is this it?"

His wife patted his arm and said, "No, honey, it's not. Because you're not home yet."

One day each of us will stand before Christ. He will praise us for whatever we did for his kingdom in this world and show off before all creation our little deeds in hidden places. Perhaps he'll even open it up for testimonies from all kinds of people who will be there at that moment partly because of something we said or did or prayed. I'm convinced we'll be shocked but also humbled and astonished by what we hear. People we never knew will speak in glowing terms of some small thing we did without even realizing it.

More than that, neighbors, friends, relatives and others will all have their chance to thank us for all kinds of things we forgot about long ago. It will be an incredible moment for each of us. And for each of us, that will be the big dream we never realized would come true. Jesus had it on his schedule all along.

STEPS TO TAKE

What steps can you take to get honest with your Lord when your grand dream goes bust? Take time to rest, to think, to pray. Talk with God about it. Let him talk to you. Perhaps he will reveal to you from his Word, or through the still, small voice, or through a friend, the great lesson he has been trying to teach you. However he does it, though, the greatest truth of all is that this world is passing away.

Only the things that truly last—personal character, love, friendship, faith, kindness—will be remembered at the end. The grandiose deeds we dream of doing for his kingdom aren't what it is all about at all.

Maybe what it's all about is just serving God faithfully day by day in our little corner of the world without giving up. Maybe it's simply learning at his feet and conversing with him on a path through the woods.

Maybe what really matters to God is you and he—friends forever.

GETTING HONEST

1. Can you pinpoint some grand dreams you have had? Have they come to fruition, or did you leave them behind, forgetting them, growing beyond them? Do you have dreams that have gone bust that still hurt?

2. God values more your relationship with him than your work for him. What can you do today that will build that relationship?

6

THE PRAYER WITH BOLDNESS
God Will Act

When the men got up to leave, they looked down toward Sodom, and Abraham walked along with them to see them on their way. Then the LORD said, "Shall I hide from Abraham what I am about to do? Abraham will surely become a great and powerful nation, and all nations on earth will be blessed through him. For I have chosen him, so that he will direct his children and his household after him to keep the way of the LORD by doing what is right and just, so that the LORD will bring about for Abraham what he has promised him."

Then the LORD said, "The outcry against Sodom and Gomorrah is so great and their sin so grievous that I will go down and see if what they have done is as bad as the outcry that has reached me. If not, I will know."

The men turned away and went toward Sodom, but Abraham remained standing before the LORD.

GENESIS 18:16-22

THE GREATEST THING ANYONE CAN DO for God and man is pray," says S. D. Gordon in his book *No Easy Road*. "It is not the only thing; but it is the chief thing. The great people of the earth today are the people who pray. I do not mean who talk about prayer; nor those who say they believe in prayer; nor yet those who can explain about prayer; but I mean these people who take time to pray."

Getting honest with God means we must spend time in prayer. It also means we must learn to become bold with him in prayer. Like Ephesians 3:12 says, "In him and through faith in him we may approach God with freedom and confidence." And Hebrews 4:16: "Let us . . . approach the throne of grace with confidence, so that we may receive mercy and find grace to help us in our time of need." In some translations the word "confidence" is rendered "boldness." In other words, approach God with boldness. Be a little daring. Don't back down. And don't be afraid. If you are in Christ, approaching God with boldness is the very thing he wants you to do.

David Brainerd (1718-1747) is regarded as one of the greatest prayer warriors of all time. If you ever read his journal, you will find in its pages a man so absorbed and caught up in the belief that prayer is everything that you will literally break down and cry for your own lack of prayer. Brainerd knew what it was to pray with a boldness and ferocity that at times seemed almost maniacal. Many times he wrote of sweating through his clothing while lying in snow and beseeching God to work.

At one point he wanted so desperately to reach the Indians who lived in the New England forests he frequented that he prayed for someone to appear who could translate his words into their language. Eventually a man did appear, a drunken lout with no concern for the gospel. Brainerd was not so proud that he thought God might not use this person, so he employed him as a translator. Brainerd then prayed fervently that when he preached, many of these Indians would come to faith. On one occasion the interpreter was so drunk, biographers say, that he could barely stand up straight and speak clearly. But he stood straight enough and spoke clearly enough that scores of Indians came to faith as a result of Brainerd's preaching.

Prayer is power.

When Albert Einstein spoke at Princeton University in 1952, a doctoral student asked him, "What is there left in the world for original dissertation research?"

Einstein is said to have replied, "Find out about prayer. Somebody must find out about prayer." What a testimony!

Is coming boldly to God something we should all do? Is being bold a way to get honest with God? Or is it something reserved only for spiritual giants?

I love reading the stories of George Müller (1805-1898). One of his diary entries reads:

> God has never failed me! For nearly seventy years every need in connection with this work [caring for orphans] has been supplied. The orphans from the first until now have numbered nine thousand, five hundred, but they never wanted a meal. In answer to prayer $7,500,000 has been sent to me. We have needed as much as $200,000 in one year, and it has all come when needed. We have no committees, no collectors, no voting, and no endowment. All has come in answer to believing prayer.

That is boldness. Lest you think that figure—$7.5 million—is slight, remember that this was in the 1800s. Today that sum would be multiplied by a hundred, maybe a thousand.

Whenever I think of boldness in prayer as part of what it means to get honest with God, I go back to a story from the life of Abraham. A fantastic dialogue occurred when God (in angelic form) and two angels came down to visit destruction on Sodom and Gomorrah.

A DIALOGUE WITH GOD

Abraham's nephew Lot lived in Sodom, and the moment Abraham learned of heaven's plan to destroy that area, he was stricken with terror. Could he stand by and say nothing, when his own nephew might die in the carnage? Abraham's little speech reveals much about prayer and about God. Listen to his first plea from Genesis 18:23-25:

> Will you sweep away the righteous with the wicked? What if there are fifty righteous people in the city? Will you really sweep it away and not spare the place for the sake of the fifty righteous people in it? Far be it from you to do such a thing—to kill the righteous with the wicked, treating the righteous and the wicked alike. Far be it from you! Will not the Judge of all the earth do right?

Abraham says several telling things here. One is that he bases his argument on the fact that God is righteous, saying that, as a righteous Judge, he certainly had to do what was right. Two, he doesn't deny the wickedness of the cities in question, but he does deny that the God of heaven and earth would ever treat the righteous like the wicked, punishing them both. Three, he offers up an actual number of possible righteous people who might live in the city—fifty—that he sees as enough to spare it. (Doesn't that say something about how few good people can keep a wicked nation from God's wrath?)

You might think God would retort with something like "Mind your own business, Abraham. Who are you to impugn my plan and my judgment?" But God didn't. He said he would spare the city if he found fifty righteous people in it.

Abraham meditated on this for a moment and then realized that maybe he was shooting too high. After all, he knew what Sodom was like. So Abraham took it a step further. He said, "Now that I have been so bold as to speak to the Lord, though I am nothing but dust and ashes, what if the number of the righteous is five less than fifty? Will you destroy the whole city because of five people?" (Genesis 18:27-28). Notice, Abraham admits he's being "bold . . . to speak to the Lord." The expression means, "I know I have no right to speak with you this way, but I have to; my heart compels me. Please grant me one more request."

Is Abraham bargaining with God? In a way, I think so. But isn't this the essence of prayer—a give-and-take, a conversation, a negotiation (if you will) in which you and God hammer out a request and fine-tune it till it's exactly where you want it? Haven't you ever done this yourself? "God, if I could have anything I want, I'd like a Ferrari. But I can't expect you to do that. So all I'm asking is, will you let me buy the Miata?" "Lord, I know I can't expect to live as long as Methuselah, but please, would you let me see my grandchildren?" None of this, of course, does anything to limit God's sovereign choice in acting.

Several years ago, after experiencing a divorce and gaining custody of my two daughters, I remarried to a lovely lady named Jeanette Gardner. After four months of bliss, she got pregnant. Now, I had always wanted a son. It wasn't that I didn't like having two daughters. It wasn't even that I would have minded having a third daughter. But please understand my family history and bear with me for a moment.

My brother has two daughters and my sister has one. Not one of my father's three children had brought into the world a son to carry on the Littleton name. I remember many times when I was growing up hearing my father mentioning how important it was to "carry on the name." And though I know he was partly joking, and he also would not have traded any of his five granddaughters for a grandson, I know my father would have loved to have had one, just one. It's probably something most people would find fault with. After all, how many people would be happy to have just one child of either sex? But it was a quirk of my family. I wanted a son to carry on the family name.

Unfortunately my dad died a year before I met Jeanette. But the idea of a legacy was still rooted in me. So I found myself praying often and hard, "Lord, if it be your will, please let us have a boy. If it's a daughter, that's okay, but I'm really holding out for a boy for reasons you know." At other times it went like this: "Lord, you know how much my dad wanted a grandson. And this looks like the only chance I or my brother or sister will have to produce one because my brother and his wife are not going to have any more children, and neither is my sister, again for reasons you already know. So I'd really like for you to give us a boy. I promise I'll teach him to play ball and all that. I'll be good to him. Won't you please let this one be a boy?"

When finally Jeanette had a sonogram, the doctor told us, "I think it's a girl. It's riding like a girl, and the sonogram doesn't reveal any of the telltale signs of a boy." I was a little disappointed, although I said nothing to my wife. But that night I went to my room and said to God, "I know what the sonogram says, but I'm still hoping for a boy. Is that so wrong?" God didn't say anything, either reassuring me or asserting that I'd just have to live with whatever he gave us.

As time wore on, my prayers became even more determined, and perhaps a little strident, although I always added, "Of course, if it's a girl, that's okay too." Maybe God even laughed a couple times. In the end, though, I knuckled under and said, "Lord, I'll be glad just that the baby's healthy. Thank you that everything's gone well, and I'll be happy with whatever sex the child is." Then I paused and added, "But it would be very cool for everyone concerned that the child be a boy."

When Gardner was born, I watched him come into the world. And when I saw that he was a boy, my hand shot skyward and I cried out, "Yessssss!"

I now look back on my dialogues with God with a little embarrassment. Who was I to ask God to predetermine the sex of my child? Wasn't it enough that I had a healthy child? Of course. But I also recall the boldness with which I approached God on what I really wanted. Like Abraham, I had tried hard to convince God that what I wanted was worthy of his notice. It didn't mean that I wasn't prepared to accept his will as best.

In Abraham's prayer about Sodom and Gomorrah, we see Abraham acting boldly again when he wasn't content with the possibility that there might be fewer than forty-five righteous people in Sodom. He kept on talking and praying. When he moved the ante down to thirty, he even prefaced his request with the words "May the Lord not be angry, but let me speak" (Genesis 18:30). At twenty he said, "Now that I have been so bold as to speak to the Lord . . ." (verse 31), recognizing how thin the ice that he was treading on might be. And at ten he concluded, "May the Lord not be angry, but let me speak just once more" (verse 32).

Clearly Abraham knew he'd entered some strange and untraveled territory. Before him, there was no prayer like this ever. But Abraham had come to know a God with a mighty heart, and with this God he knew he could ask for anything.

PRAY WITH BOLDNESS

At ten Abraham thought he'd saved the city. Alas, it was not to be. But he had tried. What does this say about getting honest in prayer? It tells us several things.

The first is to pray with boldness. Over and over God has told us to come to him with our requests gladly, expectantly, with the idea that he's happy we're there and happy to help. No request is too small or too great for him. He's the God of both small things and great things, and he has no trouble responding to each.

I have prayed both about lost household objects and about much greater things, like getting married, taking a new job and so on. Sometimes I feel as if all I do is pray. But that's what getting honest is about. God wants to answer our requests. He longs that we come to him first, not last. And he constantly invites us in Scripture to do just that.

Have you ever experienced a prayer of earnest and repeated beseeching? I think it's an essential element of getting honest with God. We come to him boldly, with no embarrassment, no excuses, no looking back and hemming and hawing about the fact that we're not worthy, like Uriah Heep in Dickens's stories. No, we come excitedly, with determination, with a sense of "I'm a child of God and he wants me to do this, so I'm going to do it, no questions asked."

Why does God even have to tell us that we may approach him boldly, as he has done in Scripture? For a simple reason: how many of us have experienced the reluctance and even disgust from a boss or a parent or a friend when we have made a request? Some people become indignant that we dare to approach them about such a thing! I think God wants to dispel that notion forever. I think he would say to us, "I will not be indignant if you come to me. I will not react with disgust or reluctance. I want you to come to me. What is something as small as your request to the infinite God? Stop thinking I'll be bothered. What matters to you really does matter to me. So come. Run to me. Be bold. No hesitation. No fear. No worry. Come immediately and don't tarry, because I'm more eager to answer your request than you are to make it!" Wouldn't that kind of attitude make anyone want to come to God with anything and everything? That *is* his attitude!

If your heart is desiring something, pray, pray again and then pray one more time. Never stop praying. Bring it all to God. That's boldness. That's getting honest with God. That's where the adventure is.

Pray with Humility

There's something else here in this prayer for the destiny of Sodom and Gomorrah: Abraham prayed with true humility. He realized all along he could not make God do anything. He was at God's mercy all the way. Several times he even worried that he might be overstepping his bounds.

But the truth is that it is humility that drives us to God in the first place. Without humility we would never come to him, for humility enables us to voice our need, acknowledge our dependency and admit our weakness. "I can't do this, Lord. Nobody can but you. Please do something!"

R. A. Torrey once said, "Prayer is the only omnipotence God grants to us." A powerful thought. What did Torrey mean? I believe God is omnipotent. And prayer taps the power of God. So prayer becomes a source of human omnipotence in the sense that we can influence God to do supernatural things in our world.

Victor Hugo said, "Certain thoughts are prayers. There are moments when, whatever the attitude of the body, the soul is on its knees." Again, a powerful thought. Our smallest needs are the concerns of God. He cares about what we care about. He wants us to bring everything to him, even the little things.

Does this mean God is a heavenly vending machine? Or that we should treat him as a heavenly genie who dispenses gifts to us whenever we rub his prayer lamp? Not at all. But that doesn't mean we can't ask for what we want.

What did Jesus say? "Ask and it will be given to you; seek and you will find; knock and the door will be opened to you" (Matthew 7:7). He didn't say ask for only big things, important things, monumental things. No, he said, "Ask" and left the direct object to us. So why not ask about anything and everything, expecting him to bless your life however he answers?

I keep a kind of journal that I write in every now and then, mainly when someone says something memorable or funny and also when God does something remarkable. Often I go back into the pages of this journal and marvel over events and situations I've forgotten. Here's one of my entries:

> I knew the tank was nearly empty, but I kept forgetting to fill it. On the way to church, with four kids in the car—Nicole, Alisha, Gardner and Kimmy Stock, a friend—I ran out of gas on 169 South. I cried, "Oh no, I'm out of gas" as the van started to cough and wheeze.
>
> I coasted to a stop at the light about a half mile from church.
>
> What to do now? I told everyone to get out. The kids would have to walk to church while I got some gas. But while I had been struggling with the car, Nicole had been praying, "Please, God, help us. Dumb Daddy just ran out of gas."
>
> I got out of the van, and pulling up behind me was a cop. We told her what had happened. She said she'd give us a ride to the church. We all piled in and she drove us to the church, where I found Eric D., who took me to get gas.

I don't know about you, but experiences like that make me laugh with a little geyser of joy shooting through my gut that God has once again done the amazing. Why shouldn't our lives be filled with such experiences?

Humility means you're not so proud that you will refuse to ask God for something, especially when it's indeed something you can't get on your own. Humility means you're not so proud that you will deny God the pleasure of providing some small blessing for you that will make your day.

APPROACH PRAYER AS A "WORKING THROUGH"

One more thing from Abraham's dialogue. It's this: all true prayer is a "working through" with God.

Most of us, when we pray, have something we want, or have something we're concerned about, and we voice it. "Lord, my daughter is struggling in school. Please help her to do better and to understand this material." "Father, my business needs a boost. Could you please send us some new clients?" "Jesus, I'm tired and burned out. Please make tonight at church a refreshing time of worship."

We need something. We tell God. He answers—gives us a yes, no or "I need to do something else first." It's not complicated. But to pray like that all the time is to treat God like a vending machine. Put in your dollar, out pops an answer to prayer.

Real prayer is communication, interaction, conversation. In fact I'd say it's like a walk with a friend. You're strolling along. You say something. God responds. God says something. You respond. You have a need; you mention it. God answers. God has a need; he mentions it. You go about trying to answer the need.

When Abraham began his talk with God about Sodom and Gomorrah, he initially had only one thing on his mind—somehow saving the righteous people in the cities. But as he talked, he realized a refinement was necessary. Maybe he was even surprised that God had so graciously said yes to his first request. But as God and he talked, new ideas flashed into his mind. New directions to go in supplanted the old. New plans formed and Abraham gave voice to them. We might even say that God, in his mysterious sovereignty through the Spirit, was guiding Abraham to ask these very things.

The truth is that true, godly prayer must become give-and-take, answer-and-response. You can't just sling things out to God like a pitching machine at the baseball park. No, you the pitcher throw to God the catcher, and he throws back to you. You signal each other. You stop, think, ponder. Then you pitch something new—this time a curve, next time a sinker, finally a knuckle ball. And each time God catches it and hurls it back at you, giving you new directions and ideas, depending on what the batter has done with the last pitch.

I found this quote in *Reader's Digest* (January 1987) from Dean Register. I don't know who he is, but he spoke this right on: "Essentially prayer is based on a relationship. We don't converse freely with someone we don't know. We bare our souls and disclose our hidden secrets only to someone we trust."

That's right. We pray to someone we know, someone we trust. So we can be bold and yet humble, always willing to keep talking and "working through." Sometimes this can be agonizing, but often it's the thrill of a lifetime.

The truth is that prayer is the most powerful resource any of us has in this world. We are in contact with the living God twenty-four hours a day. Jesus indicated over and over that praying and not giving up was the paramount principle of prayer. If my understanding of God's sovereignty and guidance in our lives is correct, God even orchestrates circumstances in our lives specifically to get us to pray and to give him a chance to glorify himself.

When we deal with prayer as the last thing we do instead of the first, we're not only cheating ourselves through lost time and effort, but we're also cheating God out of an opportunity to work in our lives. Through such prayer he will draw us closer to himself and give us amazing blessings we couldn't gain otherwise.

Prayer is not static but dynamic. It's give-and-take. It's "I think this, you counter with that." It's being in relationship. It's friend to friend, son or daughter to father, follower to leader. What kind of God would God be if he resented us coming to him as if it were a nuisance? What kind of Father would he be if when we ran into his throne room, he yelled, "What on earth do you want now, you little brat?"

Certainly many of us can act like brats at times. Some of us might wear him out with our complaints. Naturally God wants more from us than merely to be our heavenly vending machine. He wants a relationship, a fellowship, out of which grow the requests and prayers that most exactly fit his perfect plan for us. But in honest-to-goodness, child-to-Father dialogue, God is always more then willing to listen and even to grant what we desire. He invites us to come to him constantly, and in one passage Jesus even says, "If you, then, though you are evil, know how to give good gifts to your children, how much more will your Father in heaven give good gifts to those who ask him!" (Matthew 7:11).

Recently my four-year-old informed me that he wanted some soup. I was busy and didn't want to expend the energy cooking a whole bowl of soup for him, so I said, "How about some chocolate milk?"

"No," he said, "I want soup."

"What kind of soup?" This stopped him in his tracks. Ah, I had him. "How about a Power Bar?" That would be easy enough. Just unwrap it and fling it at him.

"I want soup."

"Do you mean the noodle soup in the package or the Campbell's soup in the can?"

He stopped again, then said, "I want soup." Ah, the wiles of a four-year-old.

"Show me the soup."

He led me into the pantry and grabbed one of the packages, the kind that takes five minutes to heat the water, then another three minutes to cook the noodles, then another two minutes to cool down.

I pointed to the other shelves. "How about some crackers?" In the back of my mind I heard the words *You are one lousy father,* but I ignored the thought.

"I want soup. That soup. Soup. I want soup."

I sighed and made him noodle soup.

Boldness. He wanted soup, and soup is what he got. We do it every day with all kinds of people. So why not do it with God? It might gain us the blessing we most want in life.

GETTING HONEST

1. What is your image of God in your mind—beleaguered king, bothered father or willing and able friend who wants to grant your request even before you make it?

2. Take a look at who you really think God is, and then look at the picture you get from Jesus in the New Testament. Is your image skewed? Do you need to make some adjustments?

3. God wants us to be bold in coming to him. What do you really want in life at the moment? How can you come before him boldly now with that request?

7

THE PRAYER OF WEAK FAITH
Just Admit It

A man in the crowd answered, "Teacher, I brought you my son, who is possessed by a spirit that has robbed him of speech. Whenever it seizes him, it throws him to the ground. He foams at the mouth, gnashes his teeth and becomes rigid. I asked your disciples to drive out the spirit, but they could not."

"O unbelieving generation," Jesus replied, "how long shall I stay with you? How long shall I put up with you? Bring the boy to me."

So they brought him. When the spirit saw Jesus, it immediately threw the boy into a convulsion. He fell to the ground and rolled around, foaming at the mouth.

Jesus asked the boy's father, "How long has he been like this?"

"From childhood," he answered. "It has often thrown him into fire or water to kill him. But if you can do anything, take pity on us and help us."

" 'If you can'?" said Jesus. "Everything is possible for him who believes."

Immediately the boy's father exclaimed, "I do believe; help me overcome my unbelief!"

MARK 9:17-24

THE DISCIPLES WERE IN A BIND. Jesus had commissioned them to preach, heal and cast out demons (Mark 3:13-19). Until now things had been going along perfectly. The disciples experienced and wielded the same powers as Jesus. They healed. They cast out demons. Perhaps they even raised people from the dead. Suddenly, though, their success came to a halt with this case.

Presumably this father had heard about Jesus and sought him so he could cast out the demon that enslaved his son. When he reached the area, though, he discovered that Jesus had disappeared up the mountain with three of his disciples. The father, and even the remaining disciples, didn't know what was happening up there, only that Jesus was gone. So the father asked the disciples to exorcise the demon.

The disciples tried their hardest. They commanded the demon. They prayed. Perhaps they even tried a few techniques they'd seen Jesus use—placing spittle on the tongue or mud on the eyes, taking a hand and praying, things like that. Nothing worked. We don't know how long they tried, but it might have been hours.

Now the clincher. A number of scribes ("teachers of the law") had noticed the furor, and soon a whole entourage of observers stood around the little group. They watched, and probably gloated, as the disciples failed and failed again. Some may have taunted, "Hey, you there. Yeah, the one with big muscles—are you telling me you can't help this kid?" and "Hey, this isn't even a multiple-demon situation, guys. It's one lousy demon. And you can't cast that one out?"

Eventually, when the disciples realized they'd failed, they may have begun shouting back at the scribes and arguing with them. "Shut up. I don't see you trying to do this." "Hey, I'm not one of Jesus' disciples." "Probably you people are the problem. You don't believe enough."

Maybe the others responded, "Oh, don't give me that. Jesus healed plenty of people who didn't have faith. And surely this kid can't exercise real faith, even if he wanted to. So it's just a case where you disciples are powerless!"

Perhaps the disciples even began arguing among themselves.

JESUS ARRIVES

At this point Jesus arrived and asked what the brouhaha was about. People ran to him, perhaps crying out things like "Finally, someone who knows what to do" and "Jesus, your disciples are hopeless. We need you!" But Jesus, focusing his attention on the scribes, asked, "What are you arguing with them about?" (Mark 9:16).

The scribes, of course, had some experience with Jesus. They knew, as my grandfather used to say, "He don't take nothin' offa no one!" meaning, "We'd better shut our traps, guys, because Jesus will put us in our places." They made no response. The disciples, too, didn't say anything. However, the father of the demon-possessed boy spoke up, telling Jesus several things. (1) He had brought his son and was looking specifically for Jesus. (2) The boy was demon-possessed and the demon had made him mute (which, incidentally, indicates that the possession must have happened well into the boy's life, after he learned to talk). (3) The demon also would seize the boy in a fit and throw him to the ground—this demon was violent. (4) The boy would foam at the mouth, grind his teeth and become rigid, showing that he was in a lot of pain. (5) When the father couldn't find Jesus, he solicited the disciples and they were unable to cast the demon out.

Jesus immediately responded in a most uncharacteristic fashion. It's the only place in Scripture where we read that he reacted this harshly to a troublous situation. He probably raised his arms in disgust and cried, "O unbelieving generation, how long shall I stay with you? How long shall I put up with you? Bring the boy to me" (Mark 9:19).

I've often pondered this reaction and wondered why Jesus sounded so irritated. I think I've found some potential answers. It all has to do with what Jesus had recently been through.

Shortly before this event, Jesus had been on the road with his disciples. He had asked them who people said he was, and they had replied with various answers about Elijah, John the Baptist raised from the dead and so on. Then he asked them who *they* thought he was. Peter answered with a resplendent confession of faith and understanding that still rings with power. "You are the Christ" (Mark 8:29).

Undoubtedly Jesus was encouraged by this answer. Why? He knew he had only so much time to get these twelve men in shape to take on the greatest mission in human history. Until then he'd had a tough time. Nearly everything Jesus said and did fell on deaf ears. The disciples didn't get it. True, they went from amazement to amazement as Jesus healed, preached and raised the dead. But what hard data was getting through? These disciples were dense as bricks at times. But then Peter made this great proclamation. For the first time Jesus saw they were "getting it."

The next event on his agenda was the Transfiguration. Undoubtedly part of the reason he met with Moses and Elijah was to be strengthened by the two who knew most about discouragement, setbacks and bumps in the road. Both of them knew what it was to have to work with people who were slow on the uptake. So, coming down from this, Jesus might have thought, *It's going well. Maybe these fellows really will set the world on fire. Maybe this plan the Father and I have been hammering out since eternity is going to fly.* And he ran smack into more lunacy! No, not lunacy. Unbelief. It's a very different thing.

Notice what Jesus said: "How long shall I stay with you?" (Mark 9:19). In other words, "How long do I have to hang around before you people really believe in me, believe in my power, believe I'm from God the Father? How much longer will this take, because your slowness is getting aggravating!"

Next he added, "How long shall I put up with you?" What I think he meant was "How long must I put up with your nonsense, your petty arguments, your constant criticism, your carping, your complaints, your taunts, your putdowns! How long?" In other words Jesus had really "had it," as my mom would say.

But I don't think he was leveling this at the disciples, the father or the boy who had come for healing. The disciples had tried hard, and after all, Jesus told them later that this kind of demon couldn't come out except with much fasting and prayer. So he wasn't really faulting them. No, I think Jesus was disgusted with the scribes. How dare they come here and make fun of his disciples! How dare they use their learned position to attack men who had so little indoctrination in the Scriptures! And above all, how dare they impugn everyone's motives and abilities when they knew the Scriptures as well as anyone and yet came out to cast insults at those who did!

I suspect God's greatest displeasure is leveled at those who ridicule people of faith because they may not be the most learned, the most talented or the most effective as Christians. Certainly Jesus was upset. But he still had the problem before him of what to do with the boy.

A Parent's Pain and Faith

Jesus' outburst over, he asked the father to bring him the boy. The father had probably stared in amazement at the exchange that had just occurred, all his hopes dashed by the diverting confrontation with the scribes. Now he was hopeful again. He brought the boy forward. We don't know how old this lad was, but we can surmise that since the father explained he had had this demon "from childhood" (Mark 9:21), he was probably at least a teenager.

Immediately the demon threw the boy into a convulsion. You'd think the demon might keep quiet in Jesus' presence, but maybe he thought that if he made the convulsion as bad as possible, even Jesus would give up on casting him out. We can't help feeling sorry for the boy and for his loving parent.

Two of my children have suffered from serious congenital problems. Nicole was put on a heart and lung monitor for nearly a year because she was born prematurely and weighed only four pounds. Gardner suffered from an accelerated heartbeat (SVT—supraventricular tachycardia) of three hundred beats per minute that was eventually controlled by medication.

I remember the fear I would have going to bed at night. I wouldn't know if I would be awakened by a beeping monitor indicating Nicole had stopped breathing. Or I wouldn't know whether Gardner's medication was working and whether he was on the verge of a heart attack.

The costs incurred added more pain to the situation. Even though we had health insurance, many parts of the treatment weren't covered and we had to pay out of pocket. At one point various doctors' bills had us over $20,000 in debt.

My friends' daughter Stasia was born with only the lining of her brain. It took her mother, Alsie, three hours to feed the tiny baby because she could not swallow more than a few drops of formula at once. The couple rarely won more than a few hours of sleep at a stretch, and they constantly faced new and more dangerous medical problems. But the greatest horror was the day their doctor announced, "Stasia will never walk, will never talk, will never be able to feed herself. She will be like a newborn baby for the rest of her life. And chances are, her life will only last a couple of years."

Alsie told me in graphic terms how she would stand in her bedroom screaming at God in anger that he would afflict her family with such a terrible medical problem. What hurt worse was the fact that Alsie had gone through an abortion before marrying and becoming a Christian. She felt tremendous guilt and believed for some time that her daughter's problems were payback for her own crimes against God.

I wonder if this demon-possessed boy's father had experienced some of the same horrors as have my family, Alsie's family and other families facing serious medical troubles. He had undoubtedly spent much money trying to get this son help. Because the demon threw the boy into water and fires, he had to constantly watch the child. And because of his own past sins, however trivial, he might have pummeled himself with recriminations about its being his fault that his boy was like this. After all, that was probably what he heard in synagogue and from the scribes.

A parent's heart is fragile, especially when it comes to handicapped children. Worries drag at you constantly. "What ifs" march through your mind like legions. Resentment and more guilt pile up if you're not guarding yourself, too, because you won't always act lovingly and kindly with such a child. Beyond that is the criticism you might have to deal with from relatives, neighbors, even your spouse. "You never do anything right with him." "No wonder he's like this, the way you act." It can put you into a pit.

But even beyond this kind of parental agony is the pain of the child. To see your son suffering like this tears you to pieces. I recall once when my daughter Nicole fell off her bike and gouged out a piece of bone in her shin. I found Nicole, crumpled on the lawn, crying and moaning. She didn't want anyone to touch the wound. She didn't want antiseptic on it. She didn't want a doctor to look at it. She only wanted to lie there and have it go away. Of course I immediately carried her to the car and rushed her to the ER. But that was even more of a horror show as the doctor prodded and pushed and probed the wound while Nicole hysterically screamed louder than I've ever heard anyone scream. My heart tore as I watched that happen.

This father had probably watched his son convulse and cast himself into fires daily. Perhaps the boy even had scars on his body from such experiences. The fact that he was mute made it even worse: the child couldn't tell his father what was wrong, what he wanted, what he needed. It was the kind of thing that can cause a family to split apart, to say nothing of going bankrupt, becoming homeless and living like beggars.

Into this turmoil Jesus asked (I suspect most gently), "How long has he been like this?" (Mark 9:21).

The father answered that it had been happening since childhood. I imagine Jesus' heart was powerfully moved by such a sight. Then the father said, "But if you can do anything, take pity on us and help us" (verse 22).

Of course unbelief was what had agitated Jesus to begin with in this scenario. Yet I suspect that this time Jesus didn't explode with frustration but just stared the father in the eye, saying, " *'If* you can'? . . . Everything is possible for him who believes" (verse 23, emphasis added).

I don't think Jesus was chiding the man so much as instructing him. Jesus had healed many people to this point without inquiring about their faith. In fact many times he healed and cast out demons without the patient's showing any personal belief. On occasion Jesus simply walked up to seriously ill people and out of grace and compassion healed them on the spot. But the difference here is that the man had brought up the subject by saying, "If you can do anything . . ."

Whenever confronted with a real issue, Jesus inevitably responded. He did not ignore something he knew was wrong or false or misguided. So he gently gave the man the truth on the subject: "Everything is possible to him who believes."

Jesus had raised this concern at other times (see Luke 17:5-6). If there is a main issue with Jesus, it's the issue of faith. By faith we can move mountains, and without faith we couldn't even pile up a molehill. Faith makes the grandest dreams and visions come true. Unbelief, though, will canker even the slightest efforts. Why is faith so important?

AMAZING FAITH, HOW CAN IT BE?

Over three decades as a Christian I have pondered the great question of faith. What's the big deal? Why are faith and the lack of it the lines of demarcation between heaven and hell, eternal life and eternal death? Why does God consider this "action" paramount in the lives of his people, and its lack so abhorrent?

Scholars see an answer in Hebrews 11, the chapter that offers us a kind of "Hall of Fame" of people of faith. We see that "by faith" each of these people, from Abel to the prophets, could accomplish great feats, travel great distances and act with great boldness in God's world. I think the opening verse of that chapter answers the question above. The NIV translates it, "Now faith is being sure of what we hope for and certain of what we do not see." We see a strange dichotomy in this definition. Faith means being sure and certain, yet this surety and certainty are about things we only hope for and can't see. In other words, faith is the ability to have total confidence that what we hope for and don't see will one day be real and tangible.

Isn't that the essence of what it means to be a Christian? We have placed our complete trust, confidence, commitment and dependence in Someone we can't see, who has promised us things we don't have and who will one day take us to a place he says we can't imagine. Is it any wonder many people think we Christians are out of our minds? Yet how instructive the Hebrews definition of faith is.

Faith levels the playing field. *No one* on earth can see God. *No one* has absolute proof that God can and will do all he says. *No one* has been to heaven and witnessed its grandeur. Faith doesn't depend on talent, riches, bloodline, race, personal history, age, sex, political party, corporate position or anything else we can "see." Anyone anywhere can exercise this kind of faith simply by understanding a few facts and then entrusting themselves to the One who gave us the facts. In addition, we all get the same "stuff" by exercising such faith. Salvation, heaven, eternal life, an inheritance, adoption into God's family, the Holy Spirit, the right to reign with Christ, God's love and loyalty—all of it is offered to everyone who will put faith in Christ. The poor become rich, the lost found, the untouchable touchable and the rejected accepted all through the same commodity: faith.

And one more thing: we can use faith daily, constantly, without limit. It's not a one-time experience. It's not static; it's dynamic. Wherever you are, whatever you're doing, you can always take a step of faith. By the same token, no matter what mistakes you've made, you can always, by faith, get God's help and support. It's that simple. No wonder it's so important.

A SUPREME MOMENT OF INTEGRITY

So Jesus fired out his correction, saying that everything is possible for those who believe. Then the father of the demon-possessed boy ut-

tered words that so many of us have said sometime in life: "I do believe; help me overcome my unbelief!" (Mark 9:24). It must have
taken some courage for this man to say this to Jesus' face, especially
when you consider what he had just witnessed. Jesus had upbraided
the scribes for their lack of faith; the disciples were standing about
confused and scared; and the poor child was having another convulsion. Moreover this father had just "offended" Jesus by intimating
that he was not sure Jesus would be able to cast out this demon.

The last thing this fellow needed to do was to tell Jesus he was torn
up inside. On one hand he hoped and even believed Jesus could cast
out the demon, or he wouldn't have brought the child to Jesus in the
first place. On the other hand, with all the uproar and everything going
wrong, he was not sure what Jesus would do. Would Jesus make him
some kind of example, as Jesus had been known to do with various
Pharisees and other leaders? Would Jesus take offense at anything else
the poor guy said since he had suddenly become the classic foot-stuck-
in-mouth feature of the day? And what if Jesus just walked away?

I suspect this poor fellow didn't know what to say to Jesus' words,
so he just blurted out the thing that blazed into his mind at that moment. He couldn't risk lying to Jesus, after all. And wasn't being honest
with God Jesus' main concern to begin with? So all the fear, anxiety and
rank terror exploded to the surface, and he admitted to Jesus that at the
moment his faith in anything or anyone was rather weak.

I wonder if Jesus smiled at that point and congratulated the man
for his honesty. This man had just gotten honest with Jesus in a way
many of us would avoid. This was a man with integrity, a man who,
more than many you read about in the Gospels, spoke painful but revealing truth to the Truth himself. Jesus must have been deeply
pleased, if not amazed, by what that man said.

Nonetheless Jesus immediately rebuked the demon, told him to come out and added, "Never enter him again" (Mark 9:25). The spirit shrieked and convulsed the boy again, but then fled. The boy lay there so still that some people said, "He's dead" (verse 26). But Jesus knew the truth. For the first time since this terrified boy could remember, he felt clean inside, emptied out, free. Maybe he was just savoring it a moment.

Jesus took him by the hand and stood him up. I wonder if the crowd cheered at that moment, but the Scripture says nothing about it. Jesus stepped into a house, where his disciples cornered him with questions about why they couldn't cast out the demon.

I think this is one of the grandest stories in the whole New Testament. Why? Because I know I've been that father—many times. "I believe; help me overcome my unbelief." Oh, how many times have I prayed for something, then fought a bitter battle inside as to whether I really expected God to come through? How many times have I seen people give a prayer request for physical healing and doubted that God would answer? How many times have I struggled with a need or problem, alternately condemning God for not answering and then praising him when he did?

This passage puts to shame people who tell us we haven't gotten answers to certain prayers because we don't have enough faith. How many times have I heard people say the reason someone wasn't healed, or didn't have a prayer answered, was because he or she "didn't believe strongly enough"? Bunk! I'm not saying God doesn't desire unwavering faith. I'm not even saying that struggling with the meaning and strength of your faith is always a good thing. What I am saying is that God understands the quandary and dilemma many of us face—we love and trust and believe our heavenly Father implicitly, but we also struggle with other inner forces that cause us to go back and forth in our convictions. One moment we're strong: "You will do it, Lord, I know." The next, we've plunged to the depths: "It'll never happen; give it up."

Over the years I've read about numerous people who have struggled with faith, from Corrie ten Boom to Billy Graham. It always refreshes me when someone speaks honestly and to the point: "I haven't always believed like I know I should."

One of my friends, a pastor in a vibrant ministry, once told me that he sometimes feels as if God isn't with him anymore. "Maybe I just don't have enough faith anymore. But I want to see him work again." I prayed with my friend, but I also assured him that God's work did not depend on his faith, but on God alone. God can work with us and for us regardless of how strong our faith is. Why should we think that our feeble faith would limit the power of God? To be sure, the Bible tells us that Jesus' hometown was so unbelieving that "he did not do many miracles there because of their lack of faith" (Matthew 13:58). But did their lack of faith stymie the power of God, or did God simply choose not to do many miracles because of their unbelief? I believe it was the latter. Paul said in Romans, "What if some did not have faith? Will their lack of faith nullify God's faithfulness?" (Romans 3:3). Paul answered, "Not at all!" for God will show himself true though every person be a liar.

No, I'm convinced that lack of faith is not our problem. Our problem is honesty; it's getting honest with God; it's confessing to him that we really do feel weak in faith, that we really do want to commit that sin, that we really do want to give up. It's admitting to God the truth about ourselves without embellishment. But how hard it is to make that admission at times! Even though we know God knows all, even though we understand that we can hide nothing from him, we still hide ourselves from him. We refuse to speak the truth in our relationship with him because we fear he will reject us or chide us or even punish us.

But this lone man in the book of Mark held back nothing. He told Jesus how it really was. "I believe; help my unbelief!" He admitted to God where he really was in his faith journey. And God answered with a resounding "Yes!" to his stammered and hemming and hawing prayers.

Anyone who reads the Psalms can see this struggle in Technicolor. Frequently the psalmist wrestles with the issue of faith. "Yes, God will help me. No, I'm going down to the depths. Oh yes, I will not be afraid of ten thousand people around me. Oh no, I'm not going to make it." Over and over the psalmist lays out a bleak situation that only looks bleaker as the Psalm progresses. He struggles with his emotions and most of the time emerges at the end with strong conviction that God will answer. But there are a few psalms that start in the pit and end in the pit. One of these is Psalm 88. It begins with these words:

> *O LORD, the God who saves me,*
> *day and night I cry out before you. (verse 1)*

It moves on to the statement

> *You have taken from me my closest friends*
> *and have made me repulsive to them.*
> *I am confined and cannot escape. (verse 8)*

It never gets any better and ends with the cry

> *Your wrath has swept over me;*
> *your terrors have destroyed me.*
> *All day long they surround me like a flood;*
> *they have completely engulfed me.*
> *You have taken my companions and loved ones from me;*
> *the darkness is my closest friend. (verses 16-18)*

Heman, who wrote this psalm, never emerged from his terror, fear and lack of faith, at least in the context of this psalm. It's just one long litany of horror upon horror. And he strongly felt that most of what happened to him was because God did it to him personally!

I have faced times in my life when I prayed and I honestly did not believe God would do what I asked. But often I have found that the admission keeps the prayer honest. "I sort of believe you can do this, Lord, but I really am not sure you will."

When people tell me, "I just don't believe God will do this," I always say, "What do you believe he *will* do?" Usually it's a little like the father in Mark 9: "I believe some of the way; help me to believe the rest of the way."

God will do that. He will walk with us through our doubts and fears and get us to the place he wants us to go. He never puts us down when we admit our ambivalence, our struggle, our inability to believe all the way. After all, isn't that why our relationship with God is supernatural? It's beyond this world. It's more than this world could ever do or take. It requires God's love and closeness to get us to the place where he intends for us to be.

Oh, how I've been in situations like this father! And he gives me such courage and hope, yes, and even faith. For he has opened the door for all of us to admit our lack of undying faith when we really feel that way. He's made it possible for us to confess that we just aren't as sure of things as we'd like to be. This poor, unknown fellow has broken open the truth that we can be utterly honest with God about God's heaviest issue—faith—and still survive. This man has paved the way for integrity in prayer, commitment, love for God and love for our neighbors. We humans aren't static; we're dynamic, and that's the end of it. We ebb and flow, we wax and wane, we are sure of everything one moment and sure of nothing the next. That's the human condition and the Christian condition, and thank God, nothing is wrong with admitting it. Ever.

GETTING HONEST

1. Do you feel weak in faith? Do you honestly doubt that God can or will do what you need and desire? Admit that weakness. Take it to him and spell it out. He will never reject you. Instead he will welcome you and begin working in you to build what faith you do have until it shines like a lighthouse in the night.

2. Lack of faith is not a badge of shame. It's a place to step out from. Start where you are, believe a little more for a little bit of the journey. God will take you the rest of the way. It's his promise and his commitment to you as his child.

8

THE PRAYER FOR HEALING
God Knows Precisely What You Need

When [Jesus] came down from the mountainside, large crowds followed him. A man with leprosy came and knelt before him and said, "Lord, if you are willing, you can make me clean."

Jesus reached out his hand and touched the man. "I am willing," he said. "Be clean!" Immediately he was cured of his leprosy.

MATTHEW 8:1-3

WHEN DO YOU PRAY MOST PASSIONATELY, most intensely, most with that "God-you've-got-to-do-this-or-I'll-die" attitude? If you're like me, it's when you're in pain.

Just the other day, I felt intense chest pains. I've suffered through such pains all my life. I've always associated them with the period of depression I went through during seminary. At that time I frequently experienced mild to intense pangs in my chest. I was told that it was stress.

As I've reached my fiftieth year, I still get those pains occasionally, though the depression is long gone. Usually I've written it off to stress and stood firm. But more recently, learning I have high cholesterol and high blood pressure, I've worried about a heart attack. As a result, the most recent pains put me in the hospital. I found myself praying, even with tears, "Lord, I'm not finished yet. I have a family to take care of. I have things to do, more books to write. I still have to write a bestseller, don't I?" I could laugh about it with that thought, so I simmered down, admitted my inability to force God to let me live and decided to accept whatever came.

The verdict was the same as before: No clogged arteries. No heart damage. Stress. "You're just getting stress pains," the doctor said. "Are you under a lot of stress?" With a new marriage, a new son and two new cats, to say nothing of a recent job change and financial difficulties, I guess I was under a bit of stress. But that pain sure cranked up my prayer life! I passionately argued my case with God and tried to persuade him of my desires with the eloquence of a lawyer. Is pain like that for you?

Frankly, I don't think anything is wrong with our prayers becoming most passionate when our problems are most intense. Prayer born in pain is often the most fervent, pure and consistent prayer we can send in God's direction. We get right to the point.

I think pain is a great catalyst in teaching us to get honest with God. Pain is God's megaphone to a dying world, as C. S. Lewis said, so prayer out of pain is our megaphone to God. Such prayers ring true because they flow from the deepest wellsprings of heart and soul. Being direct with God, just telling him what you want, even if that means repeating it over and over, is an important facet of learning to be honest in prayer.

When we're in pain, the thing we want is relief, usually healing. I've known people who were supposedly healed of great maladies—cancer, heart disease, brain tumors—and I've also known Christians who were not healed but continued to suffer and in some cases even died from their sickness. What is God's response—even his will—when we ask for healing?

Theologians and pastors argue over this issue. Some say there's "healing in the atonement," quoting Isaiah 53 and 1 Peter 2:24, and that we should never be sick. Others contend that God does not dispense miracles for every little malady. There are "faith healers" on every corner of some cities, and such people draw huge crowds desperate to be healed.

What does God say under such conditions?

I always look at a certain person in Scripture. We know him only as a leper who came to Jesus. In the opening story to this chapter we meet this leper—a man with a mission and a man with a passion. His conversation with Jesus reveals much about God's attitude toward sickness and how he responds to our direct, unembellished prayers. Come along with me as I flesh out the skeleton of the biblical story with reasonable details that should help us appreciate this event in all its human drama.

THE LEPER

The leper—let's call him Ezekiel—knew the anguish of a very personal and daily torture. Undoubtedly his parents had always held great hopes for their son. Perhaps he was well educated, had grown up at the feet of some revered rabbi and had learned the Scriptures. But his life's course took a drastic turn one day when he came home with a strange blemish on his scalp or body.

A godly man, he visited the rabbi immediately. The rabbi pronounced him unclean, prescribed several sacrifices and asked him to go into seclusion for seven days. During that time, Ezekiel prayed, despaired, worried, prayed again and hoped, as anyone might about such a thing.

When he appeared again to the rabbi, he learned he had contracted leprosy. The horrid word slipped out like vomit, and Ezekiel rushed home, his mind whirling with cold, gripping terror. He knew what happened to lepers in his society. He had seen them on the roads and by the synagogues, begging and crying, "Unclean! Unclean!" when anyone approached. Nothing worse could happen to any decent person. Leprosy was incurable and made one an instant outcast in a land where family and friends were the primary joys of life.

When he broke the news to his family, they were devastated. At first Mom and Dad promised to help, promised to see him through, promised to find a doctor who would perform miracles. There was always news of someone who could do the impossible, and for a price he would do it for you. Nonetheless in time the money ran out.

Soon Ezekiel could no longer live with his family. He was banished to the leper colony.

For a while Mom and Dad and his brothers and sisters came by, furtively, at night. They brought food, clothes, news. That news drove Ezekiel to crave those visits. What had happened to his friend Simon, whom he saw no more? Where was David? And Isaiah, the boy he had grown up with? Ezekiel saw no one anymore, and the hunger to know what was going on in his old world was the only thing that made him want to live on.

In time, though, family visits became sporadic. The doctors admitted, after the money was gone, that they had no cure. The friends preferred to not talk about him. Soon even his mother gave up on him. It was too hard for her to see him like that—ruptured flesh, his face half eaten away, his eyes full of dark anguish. His father told her that Ezekiel did not expect her to come so often.

After several years, no one came by anymore with cool water to ease the fever on his forehead or the sores on his lips. Ezekiel knew now that he would live alone and that ultimately he would die alone. Meanwhile he had to keep on living, and he tramped each day to some spot on the road where he had made his little roost away from the colony. There he begged, held out his scarred hand, cried, "Unclean!" so people would not come close, and hoped for a change—healing, a miracle, anything. When passersby flung him something, he hobbled as fast as he could to grab what the stranger had dropped into the dirt.

Years passed, and one day Ezekiel realized he had not felt a human touch since he could remember. He had not received a tender word from a loved one in decades. He lived as a human being utterly without hope. He watched his body deteriorate, counted the minutes of each day like the tolling of death bells and fought the idea that he had a reason for hope. He told himself, *This is it, Ezekiel. You'll be a leper to the end. Don't even think about ever becoming normal again.*

To live like that is agony personified. A person without hope is a lost soul, sinking into the sea with only the suffocating darkness to grasp him. Ezekiel probably tried to talk to God, but inside he was too bitter. Anyway, God did nothing, so what did it matter?

Perhaps God did speak to Ezekiel's heart occasionally, telling him he cared and saw everything that had happened. But that was not much good, and in time Ezekiel gave up even on God.

WHAT ABOUT YOU?

Have you ever felt that kind of despair about an illness? I have. The depression during my seminary years was the worst experience of my life. The most terrible part of it was the feeling that it would never end. That inner feeling of utter hopelessness and darkness dragged at my soul every morning, afternoon and night of my existence. I went to bed hoping only that I'd awaken in God's arms, dead but free of the inner despair. When I'd awaken and the searing feelings of depression welled back into my consciousness, it was as if I'd been lashed with a whip. Why? I asked over and over. Why me? What did I do wrong? Heaven seemed silent and cold as winter.

Ezekiel had the same sorts of feelings. Fortunately for him, though, that wasn't the end of the story. For one day something happened in Ezekiel's life that changed everything: there was news of a prophet, Jesus. A healer. Of lepers. Of everyone. Strangely, something awakened in Ezekiel's breast. Perhaps he heard a whisper in his soul: "Go to him. Find him. This Jesus can heal you."

Ezekiel started to watch for signs. He shouted out questions to people passing. "Is the prophet Jesus coming? Is he nearby?"

He soon learned Jesus really could heal lepers. Not just a thumb or a finger, either. The whole body. Fixed for life.

Ezekiel's excitement grew and resolution built in his heart. "I must find him. I must go to him. He can heal me!" The "inner" encouragements continued as well. "Soon it will be all right. Just find Jesus. *Find Jesus!*"

One day there was news. Jesus was preaching up on a hill. Ezekiel headed off in that direction, calling, "Unclean! Unclean!" every step of the way, but hobbling as fast as his tattered legs and feet would carry him. He came to the place. People parted in front of him. Some gasped. Children pointed. But he didn't notice them; his eyes were fixed on Jesus.

When Ezekiel saw him, Jesus was more than he'd ever imagined. Simple. Plain. Robust. And there was something in his eyes. Something truly beautiful. Something Ezekiel felt but couldn't express. Love? Yes. For the first time in years, someone looked on Ezekiel's face with love. The still, small voice spoke again, saying, "This is he. Go to him and ask."

For a moment Ezekiel didn't even remember what he'd come for, what he wanted. So he waited, catching his breath, thinking and then recalling when his eyes turned to his scarred hands. Healing. That was what he wanted.

He looked up and Jesus walked toward him. Ezekiel wanted Jesus to know that he was a submissive man, that he wouldn't make demands. But the way his question was framed speaks much about what this man understood in a theological framework. He fell on his face and bowed at Jesus' feet. Then looking up, he cried, "Lord, if you are willing, you can make me clean" (Matthew 8:2).

"If"? Yes, if. Consider the magnitude of that conjunction. "If" is the issue, isn't it? Ezekiel the leper believed in Jesus' power. He knew Jesus *could* perform this feat. There were just too many others who

said, "Yes, he healed me. Look at me. I'm whole, perfect, alive again."
But *would* Jesus heal Ezekiel?

Think about it for a moment. Jesus is omnipotent. But what does
that really mean? In theological terms *omnipotence* means Jesus possesses absolute, complete and effortless power. Consider one verse
from the Psalms:

> *He spoke, and it came to be;*
> *he commanded, and it stood firm. (Psalm 33:9)*

That verse was written about God's power to create. Remember
how God created? With a word. He spoke, and the sun throbbed into
existence. He commanded, and Adam was born. That's omnipotence.
It's effortless in its ability to do anything.

But what are the implications of God's omnipotence for our lives?
If he so chose, God could empty hospitals the world over and release
every diseased person from the bed of sickness in a second. He could
eradicate crime and bring justice to every innocent with a flash of his
eyes. He could bring peace to every despondent soul, lift the down-
trodden, give sight to the blind and power of movement to the para-
plegic, and end world hunger with a mere whisper of his lips. Now.
This instant. Without a pause for breath. That's omnipotence at work.

Perhaps Ezekiel understood that Jesus was omnipotent, could do
anything, even the impossible act of making him whole. But was
Jesus willing? "If you are willing . . ." This is where it gets sticky. For
other voices in a person's soul clamor for attention. In such circumstances our old nature tells us it can't be done, that it's impossible.
Doubts assail us. Then the voice of reason says, "Yes, he can do it, but
probably not to you." Next there's the devil, saying, "He won't heal
you. You're not worthy. So just forget it." Ezekiel's question is paramount. Yes, Jesus could heal. But would he, in his case?

Isn't that the question most of us face when we're in pain? Isn't that what we ask Jesus when we desire healing or a spouse or a child or success in our career? Isn't that the issue that always messes things up? Will Jesus answer? Will he do what I ask?

In that brief clause—"If you are willing"—Ezekiel revealed that he saw something else in the Jesus who stood before him: God's sovereignty. That always comes into play in any conversation with God about something as stupendous and important as healing.

What is sovereignty? Different from omnipotence, it means not only does God have the power to do as he pleases, but he also has the right—in every one, in every where and in every what or when. God not only has complete control of all of creation, but also nothing can happen in it without his permission. He is the absolute and final authority in all matters. No one can touch us apart from his will. No crime can beset us, no demon can assault us, no problem can fell us without God's agreement. We are entirely in his hands.

The apostle Paul learned that and told us about it in 2 Corinthians 12, where he prayed three times to be released from a "thorn in the flesh." God didn't release him, and Paul had to bow before the power of sovereignty and accept what God said.

This leper also saw that Jesus had a right to do whatever he wanted. If he didn't want to heal, that was his right. And if he did, that was also his privilege. "If you are willing, you can make me clean."

I believe that is the great issue for all of us in any conversation with God about anything, but especially about healing. If we are to get honest with God, we must recognize that he has both the ability and power to do what we ask. The issue is not "Can he do it?" He can. Period. He can do anything he chooses to do, within the limits of his own character. But *will* he? Ezekiel probably didn't realize all of the ramifications of his prayer to Jesus, but his theology was as sure as the sun.

I remember how, in those days long ago when I battled depression, I felt that difficulty so intensely. God could do with me as he pleased. If he chose that I go through a mind-shattering depression, that was his prerogative. I had no power to make him change his mind. All I had was prayer. "Please help me, Lord. I have nowhere else to go."

Why do you think Ezekiel came to Jesus? If he feared that Jesus might not do what he asked, then what drew him, held him, propelled him to come to Jesus in the first place? Could he take another rejection, another setup? Could he lose the last shred of hope in a headlong pursuit of God's help that never came to fruition? The choice of going to Jesus presented him with a dilemma.

THE GREAT DILEMMA

Several years ago I wrote a book about my clinical depression called *The Storm Within*. Someone gave it to a young police officer going through a harrowing time of his own darkness. He later told me it was the first book he'd found that presented the reality of serious depression and at the same time offered a message of hope. I was deeply moved by his words.

He read the book over and over. He kept it with him in his squad car. He gained hope from it in ways I never could have anticipated. But his depression grew worse. He struggled. He didn't understand why the banging pain in his heart wouldn't abate.

His wife finally called me to check me out. Though she'd read the book too, she needed to know whether I could help her husband personally. I told her I couldn't give him the magic formula for ending his pain, but I could give him the hope of a great God who could help him stand firm in this trial of his life. She parted from me, saying she had to tell her husband of my encouragement and tell him to call me or write me.

I didn't hear from him for over a year. His wife called several times in tears, afraid her beloved would commit suicide. She didn't know what to do, but she told me, "He's afraid to call you because that's his last card. If you can't help him, he feels it's over for him. Counseling hasn't helped. Drugs haven't helped. Nothing works. So he refuses to call you because he doesn't want to lose the last shred of hope he has."

I think that's how Ezekiel must have felt. What if he took that last stab at help and hope and it didn't work out? Where was he then? Undoubtedly that gave Ezekiel pause. But only a little. For there was something else about Jesus that made him think going to him wouldn't be a dead end.

I believe one more powerful truth was inscribed on Ezekiel's heart through the still, small voice, something that only God could put there. He knew that Jesus was a man who cared, who wanted to help, who longed to heal. He believed that Jesus was love personified and that even though he had the right to turn Ezekiel down, he wouldn't.

THE GREAT TRUTH

Love. That's what really drives us all to Jesus in the first place, isn't it? Yes, we believe he has the power. Yes, we know he can do with us as he pleases. But yes, yes, yes, he loves us. He loves you. He loves me.

Over and over in the New Testament we find evidence of Jesus' love—in the healings, the casting out of demons, the grand, empowering words and finally the death on the cross for our sins. He himself told us that no one has greater love than a person who will lay down his or her life for another (John 15:13), and that is precisely what Jesus did for you and me. Paul echoes the same love in Romans 8:32: "He who did not spare his own Son, but gave him up for us all—how will he not also, along with him, graciously give us all things?"

We see that love all over Ezekiel's story. We see it on every page of

Scripture. And we hear it in our hearts, every day if need be. God speaks to us in the dim recesses of our souls and says things like "Your name is written on my palms" and "I'll never leave you or forsake you. Never!"

That is what gives us hope in his hands. Love. It's not just Scripture, though that's the source. It's that still, small voice encouraging us, speaking to our hearts and assuring us of the love he speaks about in Scripture. Without the still, small voice, that love is just words on a page. But with it, those words come alive!

That's ultimately why I believe Ezekiel threw himself at Jesus' feet. He put himself entirely in God's hands and said, "If you are willing, you can make me clean." He took the chance. He threw everything he had left into the pot and hoped beyond hope that he would come up with a winning hand. Because there was nowhere else to go.

That was also why one day, two and half years after my depression struck, I knelt by my bed and said, "Lord, whatever happens, I trust you. I know you love me. I know you will do what's best. Just give me the grace to endure." God had spoken to my heart and I knew I could trust him, whatever came.

It was an incredible moment for me, for I was—in my own mind—giving up my right to feel happiness, joy and hope in my heart ever again. I was saying to God, "If you want me to be depressed, that's okay. Just help me to hang in there." I wasn't bargaining. I wasn't even asking for healing, though I hoped for it still. But I had recognized for the first time in my life as a Christian that my only hope in this world was Jesus. I had no one else. No amount of money, no bastion of scientists working on new drugs could help; there was only Jesus.

So what did Jesus do for Ezekiel? He stretched out his hand, touched the leper and said, "I am willing. Be clean!" (Matthew 8:3).

Immediately Ezekiel felt a tingling sensation all through his body. And then, as if he were a snake shedding a skin, the leprosy slid away. Underneath was pure, brown, beautiful, whole skin, bone and appendage. He was clean! He was healed! He was a new creation!

I imagine at that moment Ezekiel leaped into Jesus' arms and covered him with hugs, saying, "Thank you, thank you, *thank you!*" But Scripture doesn't tell us his response. Scripture only tells us the bare details. It's one of the simplest, most sincere conversations we find in the Gospels. Straightforward, honest prayer from a heart of faith.

At this point, though, something troubles me. For millions of Christians the world over, a prayer for healing isn't this simple. Christians fighting the horrid scourges of our day—cancer, heart disease, stroke, AIDS—find that the words above almost mock them. It happened once way back then, but it hasn't happened to them. Some pray the same words—"Lord, I know that you have the power to heal me like that leper, if you only would!"—and instead of receiving an unequivocal, delighted and delighting yes, they get a resounding and horrifying no. Is Jesus no longer willing to heal?

WHEN HEALING DOESN'T COME

Recently someone told me the story of a dear friend named Skip who was stricken with terminal brain cancer. It was declared inoperable, devastatingly malignant. The doctors gave him three months to live.

Skip and his family knew what to do. They told the church and the whole church prayed. The family prayed every day, at every meal, in the morning before work, at night before bed. People in prayer groups all over the city and country united in one harmonious resound of prayer. Many people even said they'd received a "word from God" that Skip was healed or would be healed. Skip himself felt several times that God had spoken to his heart that healing would come.

Skip and his family went to special healing services where ministers spoke of how God could help him. Everyone felt constantly on the verge of some new and awe-inspiring revelation.

But it was not to be. Skip lived more than three months but less than a year. He left behind a heartbroken wife, three desolate young children and a stunned church. What had they done wrong? Was this a case where Jesus wasn't willing to heal?

Some theologians offer an answer. They explain that the leper in the story above lived in a different time and place. The Jesus of the first century was sent to heal as confirmation of his message and messiahship. Then once Jesus was confirmed, had died and risen again, the miracles would gradually disappear.

That argument doesn't fly with me. Jesus is still Jesus. He has not changed—he is immutable, as Hebrews 13:8 says: "Jesus Christ is the same yesterday and today and forever." He still possesses the power to heal. And to speak to our hearts.

So what went wrong in Skip's case, if anything? What goes wrong in any case where a believing, praying person is not healed? Is it even right to speak about something "going wrong"?

Let's go back to Ezekiel for a moment. Let's imagine that Jesus responded in a different way. Suppose Ezekiel said, "Lord, if you are willing, you can make me clean," and Jesus said, "Sorry, I'm not willing to heal you, but I am willing to do something else."

Ezekiel would be stunned, but I'm sure he'd ask at that moment, "What?"

"I'm willing to take you and mold you," Jesus tells him. "I'm willing to work in you through my Spirit and this trial to produce the most thankful, loving, God-honoring person you could ever be. And because you are a leper, the contrast will be spectacular, like a ten-carat diamond on black velvet. I will use you to help dozens of other lepers live in grace and hope for a better world, to endure through their illness rather than escape from it. And one day I will take you to my own world, where you'll be perfect, complete, whole and happy forever. There I will answer every question you have about your life in this place and time. I will right every wrong, and I will lavish upon you great gifts because of your faith. There you will be with me forever, at my right hand."

Ezekiel might have stared in wonder and dread at what Jesus was saying in this new scenario, and I don't know what he might have said, but I suspect he might have found it an exciting proposition if he thought clear and hard about it.

I believe, if we're listening, that's the kind of message that only the still, small voice can put into a heart. If we're listening, sometimes God will tell us that we won't be healed, as he did with Paul and the thorn in the flesh. He'll let us know, though, that he'll use us in some special way that we can't comprehend at the time. What we need to do is trust him. About what? Everything.

Isn't trust the bedrock issue with God? We ask him, "Can I trust you with my life forever and ever, with the lives of all those I love, forever and ever?" That's the issue, and God asks us if we trust him often, I think, because trust must be renewed on a daily basis.

I don't know if Skip heard such a message or not. I do know that Skip's life and death were used in many ways to bless God's people and advance his kingdom.

I faced a similar problem in October 1977, as my depression raged and my despair seemed insurmountable. I'd been reading a lot about God's will and what he wanted to do in our lives. The Spirit kept impressing on me my need to "obey" and "submit to God's will" no matter what. James Packer's book *Knowing God* had a powerful impact on me, especially the chapter on God's wisdom. Could I trust that God in his wisdom had chosen this circumstance for me to mold me and make me into what he envisioned? Could I believe that God was that wise? In my heart I wanted to say yes, yes, a thousand times yes. But I resisted it.

Then one day the impression on my soul was so great that I went to my room and knelt on the carpet beside my bed, weeping. Desperately hurting from the despair and darkness in my soul, I bowed and asked God for grace to hang in there. I prayed this prayer a little later than the one I mentioned earlier, and I was trying to live up to that previous prayer, but it was hard going. In something I can only describe as an "agony of submission," I said to God, "Lord, if it's your will that I be depressed like this for the rest of my life, I'm willing. However you can use it, I'm willing. Do with me as you will and please give me the grace to endure. That's all I ask."

The still, small voice said nothing, but as I stood, I realized it was the most awesome act of submission I had ever made to God in my life. For the first time in two and a half torturous years I was able to say, "Thy will be done." It's the same thing Ezekiel said: "If you are willing . . ."

What happens when we offer such prayers to God about healing? I believe sooner or later we'll hear his still, small voice assuring us, loving us, helping us. This story shows, though, that Jesus can go both ways in a healing situation and still be glorified. If he heals the leper and us, we have a grand story to tell. But if he does something else, we still have a grand story to tell.

Of the many stories I've heard of Christians keeping the faith despite terrible illness and pain, Skip's continues to stand out. Toward the end, I understand, he came to trust Jesus to do what was right and best, even if that meant dying. God spoke assuring words to him, and he faced the future with peace.

If God wants us to do anything during a time of illness, it is what

Ezekiel did: trust that however God answers we will accept it as the good gift of a good God. "Lord, if you are willing . . ."

Ezekiel was healed. I came out of my depression three months later and have never had a relapse. Why did God heal us and not Skip? I don't know. God may never tell us, though I believe at the end he will let us know many of the secret things we don't know now. But I do know that God is omnipotent, sovereign and good. That he is loving and gracious. And that he helps us face whatever comes through speaking to our hearts day by day. I know that honest, straightforward prayers gain God's approval. And I know that living out God's will means we will face terrible and dangerous times, but his promise is always that he will go through it with us. Together. You and he. He and I.

Do you believe that? If you do, then you have embarked on one of the greatest adventures God can give—a life that is submitted to his will that has truly become honest in every best sense of the word. Your belief will make what comes beautiful to behold.

GETTING HONEST

1. Are you presently suffering through some illness or bad time? Can you look to God and say, "Thy will be done"? Can you see the "better thing" he might have for you in this time? It will take searching, a sincere heart and deep trust, but God will reveal that better thing to you as you cling to him.

2. Even if you are not suffering now with an illness, you can trust God with your life and future. Why not tell him that right now?

9

THE ARGUING PRAYER
Persuade God Otherwise

The LORD said to Moses, "Go down, because your people, whom you brought up out of Egypt, have become corrupt. They have been quick to turn away from what I commanded them and have made themselves an idol cast in the shape of a calf. They have bowed down to it and sacrificed to it and have said, 'These are your gods, O Israel, who brought you up out of Egypt.'

"I have seen these people," the LORD said to Moses, "and they are a stiff-necked people. Now leave me alone so that my anger may burn against them and that I may destroy them. Then I will make you into a great nation."

But Moses sought the favor of the LORD his God. "O LORD," he said, "why should your anger burn against your people, whom you brought out of Egypt with great power and a mighty hand? Why should the Egyptians say, 'It was with evil intent that he brought them out, to kill them in the mountains and to wipe them off the face of the earth'? Turn from your fierce anger; relent and do not bring disaster on your people. Remember your servants Abraham, Isaac and Israel, to whom you swore by your own self: 'I will make your descendants as numerous as the stars in the sky and I will give your descendants all this land I promised them, and it will be their inheritance for ever.' " Then the LORD relented and did not bring on his people the disaster he had threatened.

EXODUS 32:7-14

DOES PRAYER TRULY INFLUENCE GOD? If we don't pray, will certain things not happen that might have happened? And if we do pray, do things happen that would not have happened otherwise?

Some theologians who emphasize God's sovereignty and the idea that God has an eternal plan say, "Yes, prayer is the means by which God acts." But then they add, "Not only does God decree what happens, but he also decrees who will pray and when about those things. It's all accounted for."

On the face of it, that truth seems simple. God's plan dictates that Sarah will recover from a debilitating stroke. And God's plan also says Jennifer and Bill and Bob will pray for Sarah after the stroke. God acts on the basis of Jennifer's, Bill's and Bob's prayers, Sarah gets well and all is perfect. That's how it works.

If, on the other hand, Jennifer, Bill and Bob don't pray, Sarah won't get well. But these theologians tell us that God's plan already decreed that Jennifer, Bill and Bob wouldn't pray and that Sarah wouldn't get well.

God's plan has everything covered. Or so it seems.

It also seems as if, according to that theology of prayer, it doesn't matter what we do. God has all the details worked out ahead of time, so whether we feel constrained to pray or not matters little. If God's plan says we will pray, we will, and that's the end of it. And if his plan says we won't, then—presto!—we don't. In the end nothing I do ever really matters much, because God has it all worked out ahead of time. God gets me to pray when his plan needs me to pray, and he leaves me alone when his plan doesn't call for it. I end up doing whatever God's plan dictates.

Another camp of theologians opt for a much freer system. God's plan, though real, is not really a concern. The main concern is that we are free creations of God. We freely choose to pray or not pray, and God acts or doesn't act, depending on whether we have prayed. Our prayers get real results from God. He won't act if we don't pray, and he will act if we do.

There's only one problem: if we don't pray or witness or whatever with a person in question, that person may never be helped or saved. And so, in a sense, that person's destiny becomes our responsibility. He or she won't be in heaven because of our failure.

The funny thing is that most people ignore both branches of theology and simply do whatever comes naturally. If they feel motivated to pray, they pray. And if not, they don't. They don't worry about God's eternal plan and they don't care if anyone's destiny is dependent on their prayers.

The impulse to pray regardless of whether one can see the purpose is, I think, a good one. We have scriptural warrant to go ahead and argue our point before God. We see that kind of prayer played out, for example, in Exodus 32:7-14, where Moses engages in an extraordinary conversation with God.

ONE INCREDIBLE CONVERSATION

If I had to pick the most incredible conversation in Scripture, which one would it be? It would be the one that we are studying in this chapter. God would destroy Israel and start a whole new nation through Moses? God was that angry? And then Moses talked him out of it? Whoa! This is heavy stuff. What caused this whole exchange?

Moses had been on Mount Sinai for forty days receiving the law and instructions from God about how Israel should worship and live and so on. While Moses was gone, the people grew restless because no one knew what had happened to Moses. They approached Aaron, who was in charge, and demanded that he make them their own "gods."

The people wanted some kind of physical expression of their deity. To them, the true God was invisible and extremely vague. Who was he? What did he look like? How would they know when he was truly among them?

Aaron didn't skip a beat. He told the people to bring him their gold and he would fashion for them whatever came out of the fire. In the end a golden calf was created and the people reveled before the calf, eating, drinking and engaging in sexual activity forbidden by the law.

It was at that point that God spoke to Moses on the mountain. God began: "Go down, because your people, whom you brought up out of Egypt, have become corrupt" (Exodus 32:7). Note the emphasis on "your" people whom "you" brought up out of Egypt. God was laying this all at Moses' feet, as if he had caused the whole thing. God was not calling them "my people" whom "I" brought out of Egypt, as he did so often in other places.

God went on to explain, "They have been quick to turn away from what I commanded them and have made themselves an idol cast in the shape of a calf. They have bowed down to it and sacrificed to it and have said, 'These are your gods, O Israel, who brought you up out of Egypt' " (Exodus 32:8). Again, note the terminology: they have been "quick to turn away"—God is totally disgusted and outraged by the behavior of these rebels.

Finally, the coup de grâce: "I have seen these people, . . . and they are a stiff-necked people. Now leave me alone so that my anger may burn against them and that I may destroy them. Then I will make you into a great nation" (Exodus 32:9-10). God was outraged. In effect he was saying: "They have learned nothing despite all the miracles and great things I've done. They slough off everything I say and won't give me or anyone the time of day. They're proud, arrogant and deceitful, caring only about themselves and their pleasures. I've had it up to here with them!"

But God was not just angry enough to punish; he was so angry that he was ready to switch to a whole different plan of forming a covenant community. He told Moses, "Leave me alone." That is, "Don't defend them, don't protest and don't you dare try to talk me out of it! I will obliterate them all from the face of the earth. Then we'll start over with you, Moses, and I will turn your seed into the great nation I thought these people would be."

What would you do if you were in Moses' position, standing before a lethally angry God who can turn the world upside down at a mere word, just like he decimated Egypt with his plagues? Somehow Moses kept his cool and began talking God out of this strange plan. He said, "O LORD"—beginning with a word of respect and deference—"why should your anger burn against your people, whom you brought out of Egypt with great power and a mighty hand?" (Exodus 32:11). Again, notice the emphasis on "your." Moses completely rejected the idea that these were his people and that he had brought them out of Egypt. They belonged to God. They were *his* people!

In this speech Moses mentioned God's "great power and mighty hand," as if to say, "Hey, you did something incredible there. No one else could have done that. You turned these people from a godless rabble into your children and grandchildren. How can you be this angry at your own family?"

Then Moses tried to reason with God: "Why should the Egyptians say, 'It was with evil intent that he brought them out, to kill them in the mountains and to wipe them off the face of the earth'?" (Exodus 32:12). Moses was telling God that if he destroyed this people, it would accomplish nothing because everyone would say, 'God's purpose all along was to kill them."

Next, Moses pled with him, "Turn from your fierce anger; relent and do not bring disaster on your people." In other words, "Please, God, calm down; it's not that bad. Change your mind about this because it could have amazingly bad repercussions if you do it."

Finally, Moses brought him back to the whole history of Israel, the people whom God originally chose and loved. "Remember your servants Abraham, Isaac and Israel, to whom you swore by your own self: 'I will make your descendants as numerous as the stars in the sky and I will give your descendants all this land I promised them, and it will be their inheritance for ever' " (Exodus 32:13). What was Moses saying? "God, you chose this. You started this. You made promises that you showed could never be taken back. Have you forgotten these things? Because if you have, I haven't. Wasn't it you who said you'd give Abraham's children—all of them, from Isaac on down— this Promised Land we're going to? Didn't you say they would be your special people in all the earth, the one people whom you regard as your own inheritance?"

It was an airtight argument. Moses won the prize for diplomacy and keeping his head while everyone else had lost it.

So what happened? "Then the LORD relented and did not bring on his people the disaster he had threatened" (Exodus 32:14). Moses had just stopped the possible slaughter of millions of people. He had halted the Holocaust. He had turned God aside from causing one of the greatest human disasters in history.

Now the question: Is this for real? A mere mortal takes an out-of-control deity and makes him change his mind about something he appears very much to want to do?

Reading commentators who have written on this passage, I find several things:

Some don't find it amazing at all that God might get this angry and say these things. They say simply that God's wrath awaits all sinners who reject him. But doesn't this make God look like a maniac?

Some suggest that this whole thing was a grand ruse of God to get Moses to "stand in the gap" and act as intercessor for his people. God is using a kind of reverse psychology to motivate Moses to do his job properly. But doesn't this turn God into a manipulator? This suggests God plays games with us, simply to get us to be what he wants us to be, as if honest motivation won't work.

Others say that Moses didn't really change God's mind—after all, God is immutable and unchanging—but that it only appears that way from a human point of view. Fine. Then what that says to me is that Scripture can't really be trusted to mean what it says, but we must always submit all texts to our own theology, which says God can't really act this way and so it has to be something else. That seems like a copout to me.

Frankly I don't buy any of this. If I'm to take Scripture seriously, then I have to admit that God was seriously angry and Moses was seriously persuasive.

Still, that doesn't completely satisfy me either. For, I wonder, isn't God patient? Could God get this angry with me? What if there was no Moses to persuade him otherwise if he did get that angry? Moreover, who's to say that, even after we get to heaven, God won't pitch a fit like this about something and decide to wipe us all out? I mean, if the substance of this passage—God mad, Moses persuasive, God changing his mind—is true, then these words offer me some serious concerns about whether God can be completely trusted.

What then is the answer, and what does this show us about getting honest in prayer? I'd like to offer you three thoughts. I'm sure they won't explain everything, but they give me the ability to sleep at night.

SIN IS SERIOUS BUSINESS

The first thought that broadcasts itself from this passage is how serious sin is in the eyes of God. In a word, when people sin, God gets angry. To be sure, God is "compassionate and gracious, . . . slow to anger, abounding in love and faithfulness," as he will say to Moses in Exodus 34:6. God possesses an infinite capacity for patience when we sin as well as an infinite knowledge of all the variables that have gone into our mistakes and faults. He understands our messed-up minds and hearts through and through. But that doesn't mean he can just let sin go.

In many ways the conversation between Moses and God in chapter 32 is unique. I know of no other Bible passage in which God reveals so much emotion and frustration with his people. If you look at the prophets, nearly all of them, you find that God is often angry about sin and human iniquity. Over and over he rails against the sins of the people of planet earth, making threats on one side and offering forgiveness and restoration on the other. Nonetheless this event stands alone. Why?

The kind of sin Israel committed was particularly grievous to God. Only days before, God had spoken the Ten Commandments in the presence of all the people from the mountain. He emphasized several times that idolatry was a sin of the first rank. The people all agreed that they would follow his commandments in abject fear and perhaps even chest-banging conviction. They would do what God said.

These people also had truly experienced—more than any other generation in the history of the world—the supernatural power and presence of God. They'd seen the widespread plagues on Egypt unfold in all their dramatic intensity. They'd stood at the edge of the Red Sea as the waters rolled back. They'd consumed with ravenous pleasure the manna from heaven. They'd drunk water God provided from a rock, which we have since learned was a picture of Christ himself.

These people had all this, and yet they quickly tore up all the contracts, spit on the truth and danced and fornicated the night away in deliberate revilement of God and everything he stood for. This was akin to the sin the Pharisees and scribes committed when—after seeing Christ's life-restoring miracles, hearing his life-transforming words and watching him minister to life-worn multitudes—they declared he was from the devil. Jesus called this sin the "blasphemy against the Holy Spirit," and it's the worst sin anyone can commit against God (Matthew 12:22-32).

In effect these people were insulting God in a way no one had before or since. Is it any wonder God felt deep anger about their behavior?

Today I know people who have read the Bible and were raised on Christian truth and who talk about God as if he were a piece of rat dung. I have talked with young men and women who call God a Nazi on the order of Dr. Mengele and prefer Satan to him any day. I have seen comedians who ridicule Jesus Christ in front of large crowds, on television and in the movies, who craft stinging and heinous jokes laced with every profane word known to the English language, who induce multitudes to belly-laugh over what a clownish spectacle the Savior of humankind is. I have seen the exhibits of artists who revile sacred things in order to hurl their insults against God. I also know and have read about Christians who have committed the most atrocious sins while at the same time engaging in robust ministries that preach Christ and the gospel. The real question is not "How can God get so angry?" but "How can he restrain himself?" What keeps him from slamming these people right off to hell without a return ticket? Why doesn't he simply give these folks a piece of his mind that they will never forget in the eternity they will have wailing and gnashing their teeth?

Because of only one thing: the cross. Without the cross God would have sent us all off to our justly earned perditions, no questions asked. The cross made it possible for God to pour out all that anger and wrath on Jesus. And it made it possible for him to forgive us, offer us his grace and make us part of his forever family.

Have you ever wondered why the Old Testament is so full of war, death, rage, destruction, wrath, threats and genocides and why the New Testament speaks so much of love, hope, faith, joy and peace? I think there's one reason: the Old Testament was written before the cross and the New Testament was written after it. It's not that there's no mention of wrath in the New Testament. But Jesus and the apostles tell us over and over to leave the wrath to God. He will bring to justice all these criminals at the end of time, at the Great White Throne of judgment.

The cross cooled God's wrath and made it possible for us to experience his love. But the Old Testament, and especially this passage, reminds us of how much God hates sin and what it really cost Jesus to hang on that cross. It reminds us of what terrors Jesus must have experienced in his human form. It reminds us of what agony it was to become a bull's-eye for God's rage.

Frankly I don't think we'll ever fully understand it. God's anger is awesome. "It is a dreadful thing to fall into the hands of the living God," says Hebrews 10:31. And indeed we see that in the spectacle of Moses interceding for his people against God's wrath.

What does this have to do with getting honest with God in prayer? Simply this: your sin makes God angry. It's not so much that he would harm you or reject you, but he will discipline you for that sin. Crying out to him in confession is the first step in getting honest with God.

Have you sinned in ways that you know God must hate? Have you committed wrongs against others? Confess them. Come clean. Make right your wrongs. Getting honest with God means getting honest about sin and it means admitting it up front, no hiding places allowed.

Recently, in my church's Wednesday night Bible study, I said something embarrassing and regretful. No one commented on it, but immediately I was stung. Inside, the Holy Spirit began speaking to me of my need to repent of such comments and ask everyone's forgiveness. I fought off the Spirit's pointing finger.

When I left the study, feeling a little nervous, no one said anything and I went home and mostly forgot about it. Until the next Wednesday night. As I was driving to church, the Holy Spirit was on me again about confessing my sin. I told him everyone had forgotten about it. I said, "They don't even care. No one was really offended." I argued, "It's embarrassing. I'm going to confess this little thing as if I'd gone off and committed adultery?" The Spirit was adamant. I pushed him away another week.

It went on like this week after week. I'd forget about the whole thing until I returned to the Bible study. There, on the way into the class, the Holy Spirit waited and then struck, telling me I needed to get this right and that maybe God was withholding blessings because of it.

Finally, after four weeks, under deep conviction of sin, I brought it up at the study. No one remembered what I'd said. I couldn't even articulate exactly what it was, though I knew it was wrong. Afterward they forgave me.

Instantly I felt free. And I wondered why I hadn't done this weeks before, instead of stewing in it for a month. It was foolish. But that's the way we are with sin. We don't want to admit it. And that's the way God is with sin. He wants us to confess it, to lance the boil and get it healed. He will not let us go until we do.

I mean to condemn no one. Only you and God know what you may have done or not done that needs confession. But I assure you, if there is something on your radar right now that you know he's unhappy about, get it right. Now. Don't wait. Sin will eat you up. And sin will curtail the blessings God wants to send your way. Getting honest with God in prayer means confessing and making right the things you've done wrong. It might be trivial. It could be something most people didn't even notice. But if the Spirit keeps bringing it up, why delay? Get it right today, and you will be free.

GOD IS MYSTERIOUS

The second thing I see here is something that is always a struggle for me. I'm the kind of person who wants to know how everything works. I will take it apart to find out. But I have to admit that God is Someone I cannot fully understand. He is infinitely mysterious. Yes, he has revealed much of himself in the Bible, but there is so much more to him, infinitely more.

What do I mean by all this, specifically? Let me ask you a few questions.

Have you ever wondered how it's possible for God to hear all the prayers of people the world over at the same time? There could be millions of people praying at any given instant. How does he give each of us his undivided attention?

We don't know. It's a mystery. We're left with only one answer: God is more awesome than we can realize.

Have you ever considered what it took for God to create the universe and planet earth in all its wonder in six days with mere words from his mouth? "And God said, 'Let there be . . .' " And there it was! How can such things be? Even a father who purchases a bike for his kids has to put it together. But God merely speaks and it is. How?

I don't know. We'll never figure it out. God is just awesome. That's it in a nutshell.

Have you ever looked at the intricacy of the human body, or any other living body, and tried to comprehend how God could create such perfection—at a word? I mean, how did God know how to build an eye? The power to hear? The sense of smell? How did he know just how to construct a human being so that a person could run a hundred yards in under ten seconds? How did he ever figure out a way to make the human body all work together so perfectly?

You've got me! It's a complete mystery.

Have you ever really thought about what it means for God to have a plan for every person's life? There are billions of us, and presumably God has worked out a plan for each of our lives in a way that will make each of us a glory to behold at the end of time. How can he do that? How can he keep it all sorted out? How can he make it all go toward the end he has for it when all of us are doing our own thing without any feeling of being controlled or any sense of being forced to do what he wants? How does he do that?

Wow! This is getting incredible.

Have you ever pondered the idea that God is bigger than the universe and yet can dwell, in his entire person, in your heart and mind? How is that possible? I mean, how can he even remember me or you? How does he keep us in his mind? How can he see us way down here on planet earth from up there in heaven and care about our problems with headaches or lost keys or whatever? How does he have the time for us?

Hey, I didn't say these questions would be easy. But there it is again: God is mysterious.

One more: Have you ever tried to count the hairs on your head? Impossible, right? Yet according to Jesus, God knows that count at every moment without effort or expense (Matthew 10:30). And he knows it for every human who ever was, is or will be. Why does he even take the trouble to do it?

The truth is, it's no trouble. He just knows. Instantly. Without having to count. For every person. It's effortless for him, like us knowing how much two and two is. God knows about our kidneys, too, and our hearts and what arteries are clogged and how he needs to get us to a doctor on June 4, 2007. God knows all that and it doesn't wear him out or make him tired. Ever.

It's amazing, isn't it? God is awesome. God is mysterious. God is greater than you or I or anyone can ever imagine, even if we work at it for a million years. We'll never get down to the bottom with him.

Well, I could go on and on. The mysteriousness of God blows me away nearly every day. How can he really care about me and my dinky little problems when terrorists are trying to buy nuclear bombs to destroy a whole culture? Why should he ever listen to me endlessly bemoaning financial worries or some minuscule problem with my four-year old, when a tornado is tearing up a town in Kansas? How can he . . . Again I could go on. It just never ends.

God is beyond this world. He's supernatural. He's incredible. He's the greatest person any of us will ever know. And above all he's mysterious.

And then one more question about this story of Moses talking God out of annihilating Israel: Why is this story even in the Bible? Doesn't it make God look pretty bad? Doesn't it make it look like Moses had to talk him down off a fifty-story building where God sat, planning to start picking people off with a howitzer?

Yet it's there. And I think it's there for a reason: because it not only shows that God is infinitely mysterious, but it also shows God has feelings. It proves that just as we are in the image of God, so God is in some ways in our image. God can feel frustration, anger, disgust— all righteously.

One of the insights I've appreciated from my reading of the Old Testament is how hurt God sounds that his people would treat him the way they did. One writer said that as he read the painful words of Isaiah and Jeremiah and Ezekiel, he couldn't get over how God struck him as a jilted lover. How God sounded so hurt that his people would act the way they did. How God sounded pained and agonized and hurt, just deeply hurt.

I recall when I fell in love for the first time. Let's call her Angela. I thought she was the gem of the universe. We went together all through our last years in high school, but at the end of it I broke up with her. Why? I suppose I was feeling a little bored and wanted to meet some new girls.

For that whole summer I dated and found out there was no one out there like my Angela. So we got together again at the end of the summer.

I went away to Colgate University in New York, and she left for another school far away from home and me. We were far apart, but we promised each other to write and keep in touch. And during those first few weeks of college, I thought about no one but her. I wrote her letters every day. I left messages for her on the phone all the time.

She didn't write back and didn't return any of my phone calls. As the days ground on with no word from her, my imagination kicked in with a kind of panic I'd never experienced before. A desperation gripped me. I couldn't eat, couldn't sleep, couldn't think. She was out there at this distant school, and who knew what was happening? Maybe she'd met some fast senior with a Corvette. Maybe she'd gotten hurt and was in the hospital in a coma. Maybe she was laughing it up, reading my increasingly panic-stricken letters to her friends, all of them amazed at how lovesick this idiot was. The worries just piled on higher and higher. My imagination offered no end of possibilities, and each one seemed worse than the last. But it was the not knowing what was happening that was the worst. Why didn't she write or call? Didn't she care? Didn't she know how I felt?

At times I felt as if I was suffocating. At other times I broke into cold sweats in my classes, my mind whizzing with new terrors just occurring to me. Had she truly sloughed me off? Was she the one breaking up with me now?

There was also the feeling that she was the only one, my last hope. I'd met a lot of girls at school and elsewhere, but in my mind she loomed larger and greater than anyone I'd yet met. Somehow I saw her as more beautiful, more exciting and more entrancing than anyone else, and I felt that if I lost her, I'd never meet anyone nearly as fine again.

For weeks I felt abandoned, lonely, rejected. I couldn't study or think of anything else, and when my empty mailbox told me each day that she still hadn't written, my fever cranked up a few more degrees.

It was certainly one of the worst emotional states I've ever gotten myself into. How could anyone get that lovesick? Yet I believe it happens to people all over the world, all the time. When you're in love like that, when you have eyes for only one person and that one person seems to be slipping away, you can literally go crazy. Deep down, you feel lost inside, as if nothing will ever be right again.

In the end Angela did write and call, apologizing for not getting in touch sooner because she had been so busy. So all my agony was a little embarrassing. Later in the semester she flew out to my campus for our party weekend. I remember how magical that weekend was, us walking around the beautiful Colgate campus and me feeling great pride in showing her off to my friends. Later, as such relationships go, our love began to fizzle and we eventually broke up for good at the end of our freshman year. But I never completely forgot that feeling of desperation and longing that I felt when I thought she was slipping away.

I wonder if that is part of the feeling God had when he saw his beloved Israel sprint off into idolatry. After all, even though God has all the grandiose attributes that we study about and preach about in our churches, one thing we can easily forget is that he is a person somewhat like us and has a deep emotional life like we do. Is it possible that he hurts when we reject him, that he feels great pain when we walk blithely off into sin, wrecking our lives, and that it is agony for him to see us refuse the offer of eternal life through his Son? Is it possible that God feels more deeply than any of us can ever imagine?

I think God's heart was broken when Israel turned to the golden calf. When he spoke to Moses on the mountain, his anger was an instinctive reaction that we all have to being rejected by someone we love deeply.

Can God really be hurt like that? Sure he can. Ephesians says we can "grieve the Holy Spirit" (Ephesians 4:30). Jesus let his rage show when he visited the temple and saw the money changers. No one had ever seen rage like that about the things of God! Jesus wept when he saw the reaction of his beloved friends Mary and Martha to their brother's death. Jesus also sweat drops of blood during his prayer time in Gethsemane as he faced the cross. And what was Jesus' reaction when he cried out from the cross—"My God, my God, why have you forsaken me?"—but a gut-wrenching feeling of abandonment and loneliness?

I think we need to get it down in black and white: When we sin, God hurts. When we sin grievously, God really hurts. When we reject God and spit on his name, he hurts in his soul like we hurt when we know our best friends and lovers are saying nasty things about us.

If not for the cross, God would have blotted our lives out from the anger long ago. But thank God for the cross, because it means he will never be angry at any of his true children like that ever again!

What does this have to do with getting honest with God? Just this: when you pray, when you read and study the Bible, when you sin, when you speak evilly of goodness and truth and Jesus, remember that God reacts to it. He feels something in response. He's not a big blob out there who walks away, forgetting the whole thing the instant he sees it. No, part of the mystery of God is that he, like us, feels deeply about all kinds of things. And for us to treat him badly is hurtful.

PRAYER CHANGES THINGS

The last thing I see here is monumental: Moses changed the mind of God.

Please understand, I have read and studied about God's immutability, his eternality, his immensity and his transcendence, at least enough to realize that what I just said sounds like heresy. God never changes. His plan is eternal. Everything that he has ordained to come to pass will come to pass. End of story. Can I really think that I or anyone else can change God's mind about anything?

But for a second, forget theology. Just look at the plain example of the Bible story. It looks to me like Moses persuaded God not to destroy his people. Whether this was God's intent all along, the text doesn't say. Whether God was just testing Moses to see what he was really made of, how much he truly cared for the people, the text doesn't offer us an iota of evidence. On the face of it, it appears that God was enraged, wanting to do something to stop the pain, and Moses talked him out of it.

What can I say? What would have happened if Moses hadn't said a word? Would Israel have been destroyed? Maybe. What if Moses had opted for becoming the new chosen people? Would God have done that? Perhaps. But what might have been really doesn't matter. What *was* is astonishing enough. Moses got God to turn around, stop what he intended and do something else. What on earth is God trying to teach us here?

I think, one thing: we can influence God to act or not act, depending on our own passion, persuasiveness and determination. We can move God to action through prayer. Isn't that incredible?

It happened at other times. Remember how Jonah cried against Nineveh, saying, "Forty more days and Nineveh will be overturned" (Jonah 3:4)? What happened? The people repented, fasted and prayed, and God relented. Remember how Hezekiah was told to put his house in order because he was going to die (2 Kings 20:1)? What happened? Hezekiah prayed and solicited God, and God relented and gave him fifteen more years of life.

If the Bible is anything, it's a history of the power of prayer to move God to action. Things happen because people pray, and other things don't happen when they don't pray. It's as simple as that.

When I was first a Christian, my maternal grandfather suffered a debilitating stroke. My grandmother, a stalwart believer, was thrown into a state of fear and despair. I had read about praying and fasting in order to show God how sincere you were about your prayer, so I decided to do just that. I prayed and fasted for my grandfather's healing. Though my fasting lasted only one day, I continued to pray and try to persuade God to heal him and give him more years of life.

Over the next few months, my grandfather did recover. He lived into his nineties.

What if I hadn't prayed? What if I hadn't tried to influence God? I don't know for certain what might have happened. Grandpa might have gotten well anyway, but it's a good question.

Another situation that occurred in those days was a rift between myself and my parents about my faith. They felt I had gone over the edge, become fanatical and even lost to them. I believed they were lost in sin and were unbelievers. But I began to pray about it, beseeching God to heal the rift between me and my parents.

It was during the next year that I plummeted into that deep depression I have spoken of several times in this book. And it was then that my parents were suddenly transformed from being antagonistic to being the best supporters I had. Mom and Dad wrote letters; they visited me at seminary in Dallas; they encouraged me by phone. Dad even revealed to me a bout he'd had with depression. My father was a very private person, and I was astonished that he might tell me of such a personal thing. But he did. And our relationship blossomed. What might have happened had I not prayed?

A third personal example involves my search for a wife after my divorce. Until about two years after my divorce, I wanted nothing to do with marriage or anything like it. But two little kids lived in my home, and I knew they needed a mother. I began to seek a wife. I prayed about this much, even specifying some of the personal qualities I desired in a wife.

In the midst of this I met other people who told me in no uncertain terms that I had no right to get remarried, that it was unbiblical and that I had to try to reconcile with my former wife or else have no one. Still another person advised me to be very watchful. He said, "When women out there see a guy like you with two kids, they want to help. They'll do anything for you, and it can be a trap. You don't really see them as they are, and you can end up in worse shape than you were in when you were married." It all gave me the heebie-jeebies.

Nonetheless I began dating. The women I dated were nice enough, but in the end they didn't seem right for me. I got rather serious about one woman and then discovered that she seemed to be just the type my friend had warned me about.

Then I met Jeanette Gardner—thirty-five years old, a single woman who had never been married and didn't have children, a writer like myself. After an hour of conversation with her, I was entranced. I remember going out to my car, sitting down and saying, "God, I'm going to marry that woman." Then I added, "If it's all right with you."

During our courtship, I struggled with all the things others had told me about my not being allowed to remarry and about Jeanette having some hidden fault that would come out only after we were married. It ended up that I sought God constantly about it. In time he gave me a green light. Eight months later we were married. Jeanette has proven to be a joy to my life and my family.

But what if I hadn't prayed and persuaded God to give me another chance? What if I hadn't worked through with God the questions and concerns I had? I might still be out there trying to raise two teenage daughters alone.

BIBLICAL ARGUMENTS

Maybe you're not persuaded by stories from my life. How about stories from the Bible?

An army of 185,000 besieges a city, and the much smaller defending army wants to give up. But the king doesn't. He prays. The next morning 185,000 soldiers lie dead outside his gates. An angel of the

Lord had decimated that army. You can read about it in 2 Kings 18—
19. You can also read about it in the Greek historian Herodotus, who
thought a plague of rats caused the astonishing slaughter.

Here's another one: A stalwart believer learns his home city is in
ruins and the people are in turmoil. He's far away in another country,
but he prays about it and gets his boss to send him to the city to help.
Against all kinds of opposition, internal and external problems, and
traitorous acts, this believer manages to rebuild the main defenses of
the city, several miles around, in just fifty-two days. You can read
about it in the book of Nehemiah.

And one last one: A queen learns of a plot against her people from
her uncle. They are to be slaughtered on a certain date. She fasts and
prays and gets her people to fast and pray too. Through many marvelous twists and turns of events, the whole plot is undermined, the
people who tried to carry it out are executed and queen and uncle are
exalted to even greater positions of power in the kingdom. Read the
story in the book of Esther.

If these people hadn't prayed, hadn't turned to Almighty God for
help, would help have come? I doubt it. Those people would all have
disappeared and we'd know nothing of their story, for other stories
would have been chosen for the Bible. But the fact is that they did
pray, and their prayers changed everything.

Get this, if nothing else, from this book: We have tremendous personal power no matter what our position at work, in our homes and
families, or in our churches. We can wield something so strong, supernatural and overwhelming that presidents of all nations would
beg us to sell them the source of this power in exchange for billions
of dollars. We have a resource beyond anything in this world. We can
become part of the process by which people are healed or not healed,
businesses find success or failure, lives are changed or not changed—

all at the mere flow of air over our vocal cords. It's called prayer.

We can wield this awesome weapon anywhere, anytime, in any situation. We can use it to incredible effect whether we are successes in our business or failures, whether people regard us as winners or losers, whether we live in a rented garage or the White House. We have the power to influence the eternal God to act supernaturally in human events just by asking him to.

We don't have to beg, coax or bargain. God only asks that we ask, seek and knock. He promises answers that can be nothing less than stunning. Sometimes he will say, "No." Sometimes he will say, "Maybe." And sometimes he will say, "Wait." But often—oh so often—he will say, "Yes," and our lives will be changed for the better forever. Above all, through those prayers we can change the courses of lives, purposes, destinies and powers, all simply by talking to God about it.

Are you hesitant? Do you think I'm promising too much? I think, if anything, I'm making too little of it. The truth is, we have the greatest power in the universe in our hands. We have it at all hours, in any posture, no matter who or where we are.

We have it because Jesus made it possible. We have it because God loves us. And we have it because God wants to do things for us, with us and through us to change the course of human events for good and for glory. He wants to—no, he longs to—act in response to our pleas.

The only other question is, what are you waiting for? Get to it. And prepare to be amazed.

GETTING HONEST

1. Prayer is power, prayer is a wonder, prayer is the way to have a relationship with the most important person in the universe. How are you experiencing these truths?

2. No matter how trivial or how monumental your request is, God will work in response to your prayers. Do you agree? Why or why not?

3. What desire would you like to bring to God?